Canadian Living
Sweet & Simple

TRANSCONTINENTAL BOOKS
5800 Saint-Denis St.
Suite 900
Montreal, Que. H2S 3L5

Telephone: 514-273-1066
Toll-free: 1-800-565-5531

canadianliving.com
tcmedialivres.com

Bibliothèque et Archives nationales du Québec and Library and
Archives Canada cataloguing in publication

Main entry under title :
Sweet and simple
"Canadian living".
Includes index.
ISBN 978-1-927632-12-3
1. Pastry. 2. Cookbooks. I. Canadian Living Test Kitchen. II. Title :
Canadian living.
TX773.S932 2015   641.86'5   C2014-942345-4

Art director: Colin Elliott
Project editor: Tina Anson Mine
Copy editor: Lisa Fielding
Indexer: Beth Zabloski

Printed in Canada
© Transcontinental Books, 2015
Legal deposit – 1st quarter 2015
National Library of Quebec
National Library of Canada
ISBN 978-1-927632-12-3

We acknowledge the financial support of our publishing activity by
the Government of Canada through the Canada Book Fund.

Canadian Living
Sweet & Simple

BY THE CANADIAN LIVING TEST KITCHEN

Transcontinental Books

One of the first cookbooks my mother ever brought home for me was one of those collections of a zillion and one muffin recipes.

I was eight years old. (It was the '80s, and muffins were hot!) I loved that book. Nearly every page was covered in butter stains and blueberry streaks, and some of them were almost glued together from all the muffin batter action they saw. Hey, I was eight—I wasn't the tidiest cook back then. It was by making those muffins that I learned a few important lessons:

Lesson No. 1: Don't overmix the batter (or you'll get hockey pucks instead of edible treats).
Lesson No. 2: You can't swap one ingredient for another without altering the final result.
Lesson No. 3: Measure everything carefully and meticulously for the best texture and flavour.

But the most important thing it taught me is how rewarding it is to bake up a pan of treats simply for the joy of baking. This type of cooking is not about rushing around like a headless chicken to get dinner on the table, like we so often do. It's about taking an afternoon, rolling up your sleeves and making a sweet indulgence for you and your loved ones, purely for the fun of it. To me, that's what cooking is all about. Heading into your kitchen— together—is the best way for family and friends to bond, whether they're participating in the measuring and baking with you, watching and waiting to lick the beaters, or coming in from a cold day to sit down with a cup of milky tea and a fat slice of the moist, crumbly-topped coffee cake you just pulled out of the oven.

Here's to a life filled with happy (and sweet!) moments in your kitchen.

Eat well,

Annabelle Waugh
Food Director

Glazed Lemon Poke Cake
page 39

THE CANADIAN LIVING TEST KITCHEN
Leah Kuhne, Jennifer Bartoli, Annabelle Waugh,
Irene Fong and Rheanna Kish

W9-CQW-313

Our Tested-Till-Perfect guarantee means
we've tested every recipe, using the same
grocery store ingredients and household
appliances as you do, until we're sure
you'll get perfect results at home.

CANADIAN LIVING
TESTED
TILL
PERFECT
EST. 1975
TEST KITCHEN

Contents
Sweet & Simple

Rhubarb Sour Cherry Crisp

If you use fresh sour cherries to make this luscious crisp,
soaking isn't necessary. Serve it topped with whipped cream, crème anglaise
or ice cream for a luscious complement to the tender fruit.

What you need

1 cup	pitted fresh sour cherries or dried sour cherries
6 cups	sliced fresh or thawed frozen rhubarb
1 cup	granulated sugar
2 tbsp	all-purpose flour

CRISP TOPPING:

1 cup	all-purpose flour
⅔ cup	granulated sugar
Pinch	each nutmeg and cinnamon
Pinch	salt
⅓ cup	cold butter, cubed

How to make it

If using dried cherries, place in heatproof bowl; pour in boiling water. Let soak for 15 minutes; drain and set aside.

Toss together rhubarb, cherries, sugar and flour; scrape into 8-inch (2 L) square baking dish.

CRISP TOPPING: In bowl, whisk together flour, sugar, nutmeg, cinnamon and salt; using pastry blender or two knives, cut in butter until crumbly. Press into small clumps. Sprinkle over rhubarb mixture.

Bake in 375°F (190°C) oven until filling is bubbly and topping is golden and crisp, about 45 minutes. Serve warm.

MAKES 6 TO 8 SERVINGS. PER EACH OF 8 SERVINGS:
about 322 cal, 3 g pro, 8 g total fat (5 g sat. fat), 62 g carb, 2 g fibre, 20 mg chol, 59 mg sodium. % RDI: 8% calcium, 8% iron, 9% vit A, 15% vit C, 20% folate.

TEST KITCHEN TIP

In the off-season, you can often find both sour cherries and rhubarb in frozen form. Make sure you thaw, drain and pat them dry before measuring the amounts you need for this recipe.

Pear Apple Crisp

People don't often think of pears when they think of crisps.
But when pears are matched up with apples, they give this dessert a delicate flavour
that's enhanced by sweet spices and a crumbly oat topping.

What you need

6 cups	chopped cored peeled pears
2 cups	chopped cored peeled apples
2 tbsp	all-purpose flour
2 tbsp	packed brown sugar
2 tbsp	lemon juice
¼ tsp	cinnamon

CRISP TOPPING:

1 cup	quick-cooking rolled oats (not instant)
½ cup	packed brown sugar
⅓ cup	all-purpose flour
Pinch	nutmeg
⅓ cup	butter, melted (see Tip, below)

How to make it

Toss together pears, apples, flour, brown sugar, lemon juice and cinnamon until combined; scrape into 8-inch (2 L) square baking dish.

CRISP TOPPING: In bowl, whisk together oats, brown sugar, flour and nutmeg; drizzle with butter, tossing with fork until crumbly. Press into small clumps. Sprinkle over pear mixture.

Bake in 350°F (180°C) oven until pears are tender and topping is golden and crisp, about 1 hour. Serve warm.

MAKES 6 SERVINGS. PER SERVING: about 430 cal, 5 g pro, 12 g total fat (7 g sat. fat), 82 g carb, 9 g fibre, 27 mg chol, 87 mg sodium, 472 mg potassium. % RDI: 5% calcium, 15% iron, 10% vit A, 20% vit C, 18% folate.

When we call for simply "butter" in an ingredient list, we mean regular salted butter, because we've tested and perfected the recipe using it. Some people prefer to use unsalted butter in all cooking—and especially in dessert recipes—but substituting it in one of our recipes where we have not specifically called for it means you'll have to adjust the amount of salt you add to get the perfect result.

Gluten-Free Strawberry Crumble

An incredibly delicious option whether you're avoiding gluten or not,
this crumble makes the most of ripe in-season strawberries. Shredded coconut in
the topping adds tropical flair to an otherwise classic recipe.

What you need

4 cups	halved hulled fresh strawberries
2 tbsp	packed brown sugar
1 tbsp	cornstarch
1 tsp	vanilla

CRUMBLE TOPPING:

1½ cups	pure uncontaminated large-flake oats (see Tip, below)
½ cup	sweetened shredded coconut
⅓ cup	packed brown sugar
Pinch	salt
½ cup	cold unsalted butter, cubed

How to make it

Stir together strawberries, brown sugar, cornstarch and vanilla; scrape into 8-inch (2 L) square baking dish.

CRUMBLE TOPPING: In bowl, whisk together oats, coconut, brown sugar and salt. Using pastry blender or two knives, cut in butter until in coarse crumbs with some larger pieces. Sprinkle over strawberry mixture.

Bake in 350°F (180°C) oven until filling is bubbly and topping is golden, about 30 minutes. Let stand for 10 minutes before serving.

MAKES 8 SERVINGS. PER SERVING: about 275 cal, 4 g pro, 15 g total fat (9 g sat. fat), 34 g carb, 4 g fibre, 30 mg chol, 23 mg sodium, 218 mg potassium. % RDI: 3% calcium, 9% iron, 10% vit A, 52% vit C, 6% folate.

Many people who avoid gluten can still consume oats. To be absolutely sure yours haven't been in contact with gluten from other products, look for bags labelled "pure uncontaminated oats." You'll find them in health food stores or the natural foods aisle of your supermarket.

Blueberry Cornmeal Cobbler

This fruity creation takes only minutes to prepare, making it a sweet finish to a weeknight meal. Cornmeal adds a welcome bit of crunch to the easy biscuit topping.

What you need

7 cups	fresh blueberries
⅓ cup	granulated sugar
1 tbsp	cornstarch
½ tsp	almond extract

BISCUIT TOPPING:

1 cup	all-purpose flour
⅓ cup	cornmeal
¼ cup	granulated sugar
1 tsp	baking powder
1 tsp	ground ginger
¼ tsp	baking soda
Pinch	salt
¼ cup	cold butter, cubed
¾ cup	buttermilk (see Tip, below)

MAKES 6 SERVINGS. PER SERVING: about 243 cal, 4 g pro, 6 g total fat (3 g sat. fat), 46 g carb, 4 g fibre, 15 mg chol, 93 mg sodium, 147 mg potassium. % RDI: 5% calcium, 8% iron, 5% vit A, 9% vit C, 14% folate.

How to make it

Gently toss blueberries, sugar, cornstarch and almond extract; scrape into 8-inch (2 L) square baking dish.

BISCUIT TOPPING: In bowl, whisk together flour, ¼ cup of the cornmeal, sugar, baking powder, ginger, baking soda and salt. Using pastry blender or two knives, cut in butter until in coarse crumbs. Drizzle in buttermilk, stirring with fork to form soft, sticky dough. Using spoon, drop nine evenly spaced mounds of dough over blueberry mixture. Sprinkle with remaining cornmeal.

Bake in 400°F (200°C) oven until topping is light golden and no longer doughy underneath, about 35 minutes. Serve warm.

TEST KITCHEN TIP

If your fridge is fresh out of buttermilk, you can easily make a substitute. Pour 1 tbsp lemon juice or white vinegar into a glass measuring cup. Add enough milk to make 1 cup; stir. Let stand for 10 minutes. Stir again, and your homemade sour milk is ready to use.

Peach Cobbler

Peaches are so juicy and fragrant on their own, but this cobbler takes them
to even more scrumptious heights. The small amount of whole wheat flour in
the biscuits gives them a slightly denser texture and a nuttier taste.

What you need

7 cups	sliced pitted peeled firm ripe peaches (see Tip, below)
⅓ cup	packed brown sugar
2 tbsp	all-purpose flour
1 tbsp	lemon juice

BISCUIT TOPPING:

¾ cup	all-purpose flour
½ cup	whole wheat flour
3 tbsp	packed brown sugar
1½ tsp	baking powder
Pinch	salt
¼ cup	cold butter, cubed
½ cup	milk

MAKES 9 SERVINGS. PER SERVING: about 225 cal,
4 g pro, 6 g total fat (4 g sat. fat), 42 g carb, 4 g fibre,
15 mg chol, 98 mg sodium, 343 mg potassium. % RDI:
6% calcium, 9% iron, 11% vit A, 10% vit C, 14% folate.

How to make it

BISCUIT TOPPING: In bowl, whisk together all-purpose flour, whole wheat flour, brown sugar, baking powder and salt. Using pastry blender or two knives, cut in butter until in coarse crumbs. Drizzle in milk, stirring with fork to form soft, sticky dough. Set aside.

Toss together peaches, brown sugar, flour and lemon juice; scrape into 8-inch (2 L) square baking dish. Bake in 350°F (180°C) oven for 20 minutes.

Using spoon, drop nine evenly spaced mounds of dough over hot fruit mixture. Bake until topping is golden and no longer doughy underneath, about 50 minutes. Serve warm.

Here's an easy way to peel peaches: Using a slotted spoon, lower a few peaches at a time into a pot of boiling water; blanch until skins start to peel away, about 30 seconds. Submerge immediately in ice water until cool enough to handle; peel off skins.

Ice cream melts seductively over warm cobbler.

Peach and Blackberry Cornmeal Cobbler

This cobbler is heavenly during the all-too-brief blackberry season.
If you can't find fresh blackberries, use raspberries instead. Serve warm with a
scoop of vanilla ice cream for a homey, comforting end to a meal.

What you need

7 cups	sliced pitted peeled firm ripe peaches
1 cup	fresh blackberries
⅓ cup	granulated sugar
2 tbsp	cornstarch
1 tbsp	lemon juice

CORNMEAL BISCUIT TOPPING:

1 cup	all-purpose flour
½ cup	cornmeal
¼ cup	granulated sugar
1 tsp	grated lemon zest
1 tsp	baking powder
¼ tsp	baking soda
¼ tsp	salt
⅓ cup	cold unsalted butter, cubed
⅔ cup	milk

MAKES 9 SERVINGS. PER SERVING: about 266 cal,
4 g pro, 8 g total fat (4 g sat. fat), 47 g carb, 4 g fibre,
20 mg chol, 141 mg sodium, 343 mg potassium. % RDI:
5% calcium, 8% iron, 12% vit A, 20% vit C, 23% folate.

How to make it

Gently toss together peaches, blackberries, sugar, cornstarch and lemon juice; scrape into 8-inch (2 L) square baking dish.

CORNMEAL BISCUIT TOPPING: In large bowl, whisk together flour, cornmeal, sugar, lemon zest, baking powder, baking soda and salt; using pastry blender or two knives, cut in butter until in coarse crumbs. Drizzle in milk, stirring with fork to form soft, sticky dough. Using spoon, drop nine evenly spaced mounds of dough over peach mixture.

Bake in 375°F (190°C) oven until topping is golden and no longer doughy underneath, about 50 minutes. Serve warm.

Freestone peaches, which are available in the latter part of the summer, are much easier to pit than the clingstone variety, which are ready earlier in the season. So when local peaches first arrive in the market, stick to eating them out of hand and wait until later to make pies, crumbles and cobblers.

Saskatoon Berry Cobbler

Deliciously fruity, with a taste similar to that of blueberries,
saskatoon berries make an excellent cobbler base. They're naturally sweet and juicy,
so they don't require the addition of a lot of sugar.

What you need

3 tbsp	all-purpose flour
½ cup	cold water
5 cups	fresh or thawed frozen saskatoon berries (see Tip, below)
⅓ cup	granulated sugar
	Grated zest and juice of 1 lemon
1 tbsp	butter

BISCUIT TOPPING:

1 cup	all-purpose flour
⅓ cup	granulated sugar
2 tsp	baking powder
¼ tsp	salt
3 tbsp	cold butter, cubed
½ cup	milk
1 tsp	turbinado or granulated sugar

MAKES 9 SERVINGS. PER SERVING: about 233 cal,
3 g pro, 6 g total fat (4 g sat. fat), 43 g carb, 5 g fibre,
15 mg chol, 174 mg sodium, 170 mg potassium. % RDI:
8% calcium, 11% iron, 6% vit A, 8% vit C, 17% folate.

How to make it

Stir flour with ¼ cup of the cold water; set aside.
In saucepan, combine 2 cups of the saskatoon berries,
the sugar, lemon zest, lemon juice and remaining cold
water. Bring to boil; reduce heat to medium and cook
just until berries start to break down, about 3 minutes.
Stir in flour mixture; cook, stirring, until thickened,
1 to 2 minutes.

Remove from heat; stir in remaining berries and butter;
scrape into 8-inch (2 L) square baking dish.

BISCUIT TOPPING: In large bowl, whisk together
flour, granulated sugar, baking powder and salt. Using
pastry blender or two knives, cut in butter until in coarse
crumbs. Drizzle in milk, stirring with fork to form soft,
sticky dough. Using spoon, drop nine evenly spaced
mounds of dough over berry mixture. Sprinkle with
turbinado sugar.

Bake in 400°F (200°C) oven until topping is golden
and no longer doughy underneath, 20 to 25 minutes.
Serve warm.

Saskatoon berries are a regional specialty that grows in the western part of Canada.
Some berry farms in other provinces cultivate them too, so you may be able to buy them
across the country. Frozen berries work well if you can't find fresh, and you can substitute
blueberries if you can't find either fresh or frozen saskatoon berries.

Plum Berry Grunt

Grunts (or slumps) are stewed fruit puddings topped with dumplings made
of biscuit dough. Some say the odd name comes from the sound the fruit makes as it cooks.
We've updated ours by adding hazelnuts to the dumplings.

What you need

900 g	plums (about 12), pitted and sliced
1 cup	each fresh raspberries, blackberries and blueberries
¾ cup	granulated sugar (approx)
2 tsp	cornstarch
2 tbsp	lemon juice

DUMPLINGS:

¼ cup	hazelnuts
½ cup	all-purpose flour
¼ cup	spelt or whole wheat flour
3 tbsp	granulated sugar
2 tsp	baking powder
¼ tsp	salt
¼ cup	cold unsalted butter, cubed
½ cup	milk

MAKES 8 SERVINGS. PER SERVING: about 310 cal,
4 g pro, 10 g total fat (4 g sat. fat), 56 g carb, 5 g fibre,
16 mg chol, 156 mg sodium, 303 mg potassium. % RDI:
7% calcium, 6% iron, 9% vit A, 23% vit C, 12% folate.

How to make it

DUMPLINGS: On rimmed baking sheet, toast hazelnuts in 350°F (180°C) oven until lightly browned, about 10 minutes. Transfer to towel; rub off as much of the skins as possible. In food processor, pulse hazelnuts until coarsely ground.

In large bowl, whisk together all-purpose flour, spelt flour, hazelnuts, sugar, baking powder and salt. Using pastry blender or two knives, cut in butter until in coarse crumbs. Drizzle in milk, stirring with fork to form soft, sticky dough. Set aside.

Toss together plums, raspberries, blackberries, blueberries, sugar and cornstarch, adding up to 2 tbsp more sugar for tart berries, if desired. Transfer to shallow Dutch oven.

Add ½ cup water and lemon juice to fruit mixture; bring to boil over medium heat. Reduce heat, cover and simmer for 10 minutes, without lifting lid.

Drop dumplings by spoonfuls onto fruit mixture. Cover and simmer over low heat until dumplings are firm to the touch and no longer doughy underneath, 15 to 20 minutes. Serve warm.

Peach Betty

Brown Betties, or Betties, are puddings of fruit tossed with sugar and spices, and layered with buttered crumbs. They are homey looking and tasting—and dead simple to make.

What you need

2 cups	coarse fresh bread crumbs (see Tip, below)
¼ cup	butter, melted
8 cups	thickly sliced pitted peeled peaches (see Tip, page 14)
⅔ cup	packed brown sugar
½ tsp	grated lemon zest
Pinch	each nutmeg and cinnamon
2 tsp	lemon juice

How to make it

Toss bread crumbs with butter; spread one-quarter in 8-inch (2 L) square baking dish.

Toss together peaches, brown sugar, lemon zest, nutmeg and cinnamon; spread half over crumb mixture in baking dish. Top with another quarter of the crumb mixture; spread remaining peach mixture over top. Drizzle with 3 tbsp water and lemon juice. Sprinkle with remaining crumb mixture.

Bake in 375°F (190°C) oven until topping is golden and fruit is tender, about 45 minutes. Serve warm.

MAKES 8 SERVINGS. PER SERVING: about 215 cal, 3 g pro, 7 g total fat (4 g sat. fat), 40 g carb, 4 g fibre, 15 mg chol, 105 mg sodium, 403 mg potassium. % RDI: 4% calcium, 8% iron, 11% vit A, 20% vit C, 8% folate.

TEST KITCHEN TIP Coarse fresh bread crumbs are simple to make. Cut up crusty bread—day-old works very well—and whirl in a food processor until in coarse crumbs. If you make more than you need for this recipe, the crumbs freeze well for use in other dishes.

Apple Brown Betty

This rustic indulgence is easy enough to make that you can even serve it on a busy weeknight.
Let it bake while you eat dinner, and enjoy it warm right out of the oven.

What you need

6	apples (about 1.125 kg), see Tip, below
¼ cup	apple cider or juice
1 tbsp	lemon juice
¾ cup	dried bread crumbs
½ cup	packed brown sugar
¼ cup	unsalted butter, melted
¾ tsp	cinnamon
Pinch	each nutmeg and ground allspice
	Vanilla yogurt or vanilla frozen yogurt (optional)

How to make it

Peel and core apples; cut into ¼-inch (5 mm) thick slices. Toss together apples, cider and lemon juice; scrape into 8-inch (2 L) square baking dish.

Toss together bread crumbs, brown sugar, butter, cinnamon, nutmeg and allspice; sprinkle over apple mixture. Cover with foil. Bake in 350°F (180°C) oven just until tender, about 45 minutes.

Uncover and bake until filling is bubbly and topping is golden and crisp, about 20 minutes. Serve warm, with yogurt (if using).

MAKES 4 SERVINGS. PER SERVING: about 401 cal,
4 g pro, 13 g total fat (8 g sat. fat), 72 g carb, 4 g fibre,
30 mg chol, 162 mg sodium. % RDI: 7% calcium, 14% iron,
11% vit A, 12% vit C, 10% folate.

TEST KITCHEN TIP

Certain apples hold their shape better in baking than others. Some of our favourites for cooking are Golden Delicious, Honeycrisp, Braeburn and Jonagold. McIntosh and other soft (not crispy) apples will break down when heated, making them better suited for applesauce.

Nectarine and Cherry Brown Betty

Challah, or egg bread, adds a fresh twist to an old-fashioned brown Betty. For ultimate crispness, enjoy this classic right away. You can make it into a cobbler using your favourite cobbler dough; just omit the hot water in the filling and add 2 tbsp all-purpose flour to the fruit.

What you need

6 cups	sliced pitted nectarines
2 cups	pitted fresh sweet cherries
⅓ cup	packed brown sugar
2 tsp	finely grated lemon zest
2 tsp	lemon juice
½ tsp	cinnamon
Pinch	each salt and ground allspice
⅔ cup	hot water

TOPPING:

5 cups	torn egg bread or challah (about 7 slices)
½ cup	unsalted butter, melted

MAKES 8 SERVINGS. PER SERVING: about 305 cal, 5 g pro, 14 g total fat (8 g sat. fat), 42 g carb, 3 g fibre, 49 mg chol, 180 mg sodium, 359 mg potassium. % RDI: 5% calcium, 12% iron, 13% vit A, 12% vit C, 15% folate.

How to make it

TOPPING: In food processor, pulse bread until in fine crumbs to make 3 cups. Spread on rimmed baking sheet; bake in 350°F (180°C) oven, stirring a few times, until light golden and dry, about 5 minutes. Let cool.

Toss bread crumbs with butter; spread one-quarter in 8-inch (2 L) square baking dish.

Toss together nectarines, cherries, brown sugar, lemon zest, lemon juice, cinnamon, salt and allspice. Spread half over crumb mixture in dish. Top with another quarter of the crumb mixture; spread remaining nectarine mixture over top. Sprinkle with remaining crumb mixture; drizzle with hot water.

Cover with foil; bake in 350°F (180°C) oven for 40 minutes. Uncover and bake until fruit is tender and topping is golden and crisp, about 25 minutes. Serve warm.

CHANGE IT UP

Nectarine and Cherry Brown Betty With Raisin Bread Topping

TOPPING: Add ¼ cup raisins, and pinch each cinnamon and salt when tossing bread crumbs with butter.

Try tangy crème fraîche on
a sweet Betty.

Apple Raisin Pandowdy

A pandowdy is like a deep-dish fruit pie with a biscuit topping
that bakes into a flaky crust. Serve at room temperature or warm (with ice cream),
breaking the crust into the fruit when serving.

What you need

½ cup	raisins
¼ cup	rum or brandy
8 cups	sliced cored peeled apples
⅓ cup	granulated sugar
2 tbsp	all-purpose flour
½ tsp	each cinnamon and ground ginger
Pinch	each ground cloves and nutmeg
1	egg yolk
2 tsp	coarse or granulated sugar

PASTRY:

1¼ cups	all-purpose flour
¼ tsp	salt
¼ cup	cold unsalted butter, cubed
¼ cup	cold lard, cubed
2 tbsp	ice water (approx)
1½ tbsp	10% cream or milk
½ tsp	lemon juice or white vinegar

MAKES 8 SERVINGS. PER SERVING: about 320 cal,
3 g pro, 14 g total fat (7 g sat. fat), 47 g carb, 3 g fibre,
48 mg chol, 76 mg sodium, 200 mg potassium. % RDI:
2% calcium, 10% iron, 7% vit A, 5% vit C, 22% folate.

How to make it

PASTRY: In large bowl, whisk flour with salt. Using pastry blender or two knives, cut in butter and lard until in fine crumbs with a few larger pieces. Whisk together ice water, cream and lemon juice; drizzle over flour mixture, tossing briskly with fork and adding a little more water if necessary to form ragged dough. Press into disc. Wrap and refrigerate until chilled, about 30 minutes.

Meanwhile, in microwaveable bowl, stir raisins with rum. Microwave on high for 1 minute. Let stand for 15 minutes.

Toss together apples, raisin mixture, sugar, flour, cinnamon, ginger, cloves and nutmeg; scrape into 8-inch (2 L) square baking dish.

On lightly floured surface, roll out pastry into 10½-inch (26 cm) square; lay over fruit. Trim edges to extend ½ inch (1 cm) beyond edges of dish. Flute edges, tucking inside rim of dish. Whisk egg yolk with 1 tsp water; brush over pastry. Sprinkle with coarse sugar. Cut steam vents in top.

Bake in 400°F (200°C) oven for 20 minutes. Reduce heat to 350°F (180°C); bake until pastry is golden, about 25 minutes. Serve warm.

Gooseberry Pandowdy

Early gooseberries are green, tart and not very juicy, so you'll need to add 2 tbsp water to the fruit. Red gooseberries are softer and sweeter; the extra water is not needed, and you can reduce the amount of sugar in the filling by 2 tbsp if you prefer a sweet-tart result.

What you need

4 cups	gooseberries, topped and tailed (see Tip, below)
1 cup	granulated sugar
2 tbsp	tapioca flour or cornstarch
1	egg yolk
2 tsp	coarse or granulated sugar

PASTRY:

1¼ cups	all-purpose flour
¼ tsp	salt
¼ cup	cold unsalted butter, cubed
¼ cup	cold lard, cubed
2 tbsp	ice water (approx)
1½ tbsp	10% cream or milk
½ tsp	lemon juice or white vinegar

How to make it

PASTRY: In large bowl, whisk flour with salt. Using pastry blender or two knives, cut in butter and lard until in fine crumbs with a few larger pieces. Whisk together ice water, cream and lemon juice; drizzle over flour mixture, tossing briskly with fork and adding a little more water if necessary to form ragged dough. Press into disc. Wrap and refrigerate until chilled, about 30 minutes.

Toss together gooseberries, sugar and flour, adding 2 tbsp water if using green gooseberries. Scrape into 9-inch (23 cm) pie plate.

On lightly floured surface, roll out pastry into 10½-inch (26 cm) circle; lay over fruit. Trim edge to extend ½ inch (1 cm) beyond edge of dish. Flute edge, tucking inside rim of dish. Whisk egg yolk with 1 tsp water; brush over pastry. Sprinkle with coarse sugar. Cut steam vents in top.

Bake in 400°F (200°C) oven for 20 minutes. Reduce heat to 350°F (180°C); bake until pastry is golden, about 25 minutes. Let cool in pan on rack for 20 minutes.

MAKES 8 SERVINGS. PER SERVING: about 333 cal, 3 g pro, 14 g total fat (7 g sat. fat), 51 g carb, 4 g fibre, 48 mg chol, 76 mg sodium, 178 mg potassium. % RDI: 3% calcium, 9% iron, 8% vit A, 25% vit C, 21% folate.

Topping and tailing a gooseberry means cutting off the stem and flower ends that stick out of the berry. Use a sharp pair of kitchen scissors to make the job go quickly.

Gooey caramel makes
any cake glorious.

Upside-Down Buttermilk Pear Cake

Delicate slices of pear and a rich, gooey caramel sauce are the crowning glories of this rustic cake. Pears that are firm and ripe should be very fragrant.

What you need

½ cup	packed brown sugar
¼ cup	unsalted butter
2 tsp	lemon juice
3	firm ripe pears (about 565 g)

BUTTERMILK CAKE:

½ cup	unsalted butter, softened
⅓ cup	granulated sugar
⅓ cup	packed brown sugar
2	eggs
1 tsp	vanilla
1⅓ cups	all-purpose flour
1½ tsp	baking powder
½ tsp	baking soda
Pinch	salt
¾ cup	buttermilk

MAKES 12 SERVINGS. PER SERVING: about 274 cal, 3 g pro, 13 g total fat (8 g sat. fat), 38 g carb, 2 g fibre, 63 mg chol, 122 mg sodium, 155 mg potassium. % RDI: 6% calcium, 8% iron, 12% vit A, 2% vit C, 16% folate.

How to make it

In saucepan over medium heat, cook brown sugar, butter and lemon juice, stirring, until sugar is dissolved, about 2 minutes. Scrape into parchment paper–lined 9-inch (2.5 L) square cake pan.

Peel, core and halve pears; cut each half into about ¼-inch (5 mm) thick wedges. Arrange wedges, overlapping slightly, in pan.

BUTTERMILK CAKE: In large bowl, beat together butter, granulated sugar and brown sugar until fluffy; beat in eggs and vanilla.

Whisk together flour, baking powder, baking soda and salt; stir into butter mixture alternately with buttermilk, making three additions of dry ingredients and two of buttermilk. Pour over pears, smoothing to edges of pan.

Bake in 350°F (180°C) oven until cake tester inserted in centre comes out clean, about 40 minutes. Let cool in pan on rack for 10 minutes. Invert onto serving plate; peel off parchment paper.

TEST KITCHEN TIP

If any of the caramel-and-pear topping sticks to the parchment paper, don't worry. Use the tip of a sharp knife to scrape it back onto the top of the cake.

Raspberry Upside-Down Cake

Bring back a retro classic with this seasonal upside-down cake. It's delicious served warm or at room temperature. The simple glaze gives it a quick yet special finish.

What you need

½ cup	butter, softened
⅓ cup	granulated sugar
⅓ cup	packed brown sugar
2	eggs
1 tsp	vanilla
1¾ cups	all-purpose flour
1½ tsp	baking powder
½ tsp	baking soda
¾ cup	milk
½ cup	icing sugar

RASPBERRY CARAMEL TOPPING:

½ cup	packed brown sugar
¼ cup	butter
2	pkg (each 170 g) fresh raspberries (see Tip, below)

MAKES 12 SERVINGS. PER SERVING: about 302 cal, 4 g pro, 13 g total fat (8 g sat. fat), 43 g carb, 2 g fibre, 62 mg chol, 195 mg sodium, 117 mg potassium. % RDI: 6% calcium, 9% iron, 13% vit A, 12% vit C, 17% folate.

How to make it

RASPBERRY CARAMEL TOPPING: In saucepan over medium heat, cook brown sugar, butter and 1 tsp water, stirring, until sugar is dissolved, about 2 minutes. Scrape into parchment paper–lined 9-inch (2.5 L) square cake pan. Arrange raspberries on top of sugar mixture.

In large bowl, beat together butter, granulated sugar and brown sugar until fluffy; beat in eggs and vanilla.

Whisk together flour, baking powder and baking soda. Stir into butter mixture alternately with milk, making three additions of dry ingredients and two of milk. Pour over raspberries, smoothing to edges of pan.

Bake in 350°F (180°C) oven until cake tester inserted in centre comes out clean, about 35 minutes. Let cool in pan on rack for 10 minutes.

Meanwhile, mix icing sugar with 2 tsp water until smooth. Invert warm cake onto serving plate; peel off parchment paper. Drizzle with icing.

TEST KITCHEN TIP

Raspberries are quite delicate and can spoil easily. Keep them for only a day or two in the refrigerator, and don't wash them until just before you're ready to use them.

Rustic Apple Cake

There is just enough batter to hold the apples together in this French-style cake.
You can use any baking apple you like; simply make sure it is a variety
that will maintain its shape when cooked.

What you need

4	baking apples (about 900 g), see Tip, page 23
½ cup	all-purpose flour
⅓ cup	granulated sugar
1 tbsp	baking powder
½ tsp	grated lemon zest
¼ tsp	salt
⅓ cup	milk
2	eggs
2 tbsp	butter, melted and cooled
½ tsp	vanilla
1 tbsp	icing sugar

How to make it

Grease 9-inch (2.5 L) springform pan; line bottom with parchment paper. Set aside.

Peel, quarter and core apples; slice crosswise into scant ⅛-inch (3 mm) thick slices. Set aside.

In large bowl, whisk together flour, sugar, baking powder, lemon zest and salt.

Whisk together milk, eggs, butter and vanilla; pour over dry ingredients and stir gently to combine. Fold in apples. Pour into prepared pan.

Bake in 425°F (220°C) oven until top is puffed, golden and firm to the touch, about 40 minutes. Run knife around edge of cake; let cool in pan on rack for 10 minutes.

Release side of pan from around cake; let cool completely. Dust with icing sugar just before serving.

MAKES 10 TO 12 SERVINGS. PER EACH OF 12 SERVINGS:
about 105 cal, 2 g pro, 3 g total fat (2 g sat. fat), 18 g carb, 1 g fibre,
36 mg chol, 150 mg sodium, 80 mg potassium. % RDI: 5% calcium,
4% iron, 4% vit A, 3% vit C, 5% folate.

Steamed Pumpkin Cakes With Brown Sugar Sauce

Old-fashioned sticky date pudding gets a makeover with pumpkin purée.
Brandy makes the dates moist and gives them a bit of zing.

What you need

1 cup	chopped pitted dates (see Tip, page 65)
¼ cup	brandy or boiling water
1 cup	fresh bread crumbs
½ cup	butter, softened
½ cup	packed brown sugar
2	eggs
1 cup	canned pumpkin purée (see Tip, page 88)
1¼ cups	all-purpose flour
1 tsp	baking powder
¼ tsp	each ground ginger and nutmeg
Pinch	each ground cloves and salt

BROWN SUGAR SAUCE:

⅔ cup	packed brown sugar
⅔ cup	whipping cream (35%)
¼ cup	butter

MAKES 6 SERVINGS. PER SERVING: about 691 cal, 7 g pro,
35 g total fat (21 g sat. fat), 91 g carb, 5 g fibre, 157 mg chol,
302 mg sodium, 514 mg potassium. % RDI: 11% calcium, 24% iron,
112% vit A, 3% vit C, 35% folate.

How to make it

In bowl, soak dates in brandy for 1 hour or up to 24 hours.
Stir in bread crumbs; set aside.

In large bowl, beat butter with brown sugar until fluffy;
beat in eggs, one at a time, beating well after each. Beat
in pumpkin purée.

Whisk together flour, baking powder, ginger, nutmeg,
cloves and salt; stir into butter mixture. Stir in date
mixture. Divide among six greased 6-oz (175 mL)
ramekins, smoothing tops. Place circle of parchment
paper directly on surface of each. Cover each with
double-thickness foil; press down side.

Place ramekins on rack in roasting pan; pour in enough
boiling water to come halfway up sides of ramekins.
Cover pan with foil; bring to boil. Reduce heat and
simmer until skewer inserted into centre of each comes
out clean, about 1 hour.

Remove ramekins from water; remove foil and parchment
paper. Let stand for 10 minutes. Run knife around edges
to loosen; turn out onto plates. *(Make-ahead: Let cool.
Wrap individually and refrigerate for up to 24 hours; reheat
in microwave.)*

BROWN SUGAR SAUCE: In saucepan, bring brown
sugar, cream and butter to boil; reduce heat and simmer
for 3 minutes. Stir until smooth. Serve with cakes.

Victorian Tea Cake

This gorgeous yet simple British classic is a delightful treat with a proper cuppa,
but it also makes a wonderful dessert to share with friends.

What you need

½ cup	unsalted butter, softened
1 cup	granulated sugar
2	eggs, at room temperature
½ tsp	vanilla
1¾ cups	sifted cake-and-pastry flour
1½ tsp	baking powder
Pinch	salt
½ cup	milk
	Icing sugar

FILLING:

⅔ cup	whipping cream (35%)
½ cup	strawberry jam

How to make it

Grease and flour 8- or 9-inch (1.2 or 1.5 L) round cake pan; line bottom with parchment paper. Set aside.

In large bowl, beat butter until light and pale, about 2 minutes. Beat in sugar, 3 tbsp at a time, beating for 30 seconds after each addition, about 3 minutes total. Beat in eggs, one at a time, beating well after each. Beat in vanilla.

Whisk together flour, baking powder and salt; sift into butter mixture alternately with milk, making three additions of dry ingredients and two of milk. Scrape into prepared pan; smooth top.

Bake in 350°F (180°C) oven until cake tester inserted in centre comes out clean, 30 to 35 minutes. Let cool in pan on rack for 10 minutes. Turn out onto rack; peel off parchment paper. Let cool.

FILLING: In bowl, whip cream. Invert cake onto platter. Using long serrated knife, cut in half horizontally. Spread cut side of bottom layer with jam; top with whipped cream. Replace top of cake. Sift icing sugar over top.

MAKES 10 TO 12 SERVINGS. PER EACH OF 12 SERVINGS:
about 291 cal, 3 g pro, 14 g total fat (8 g sat. fat), 40 g carb, trace fibre, 69 mg chol, 63 mg sodium, 67 mg potassium. % RDI: 4% calcium, 10% iron, 14% vit A, 2% vit C, 12% folate.

A sifter is a handy little device to have on hand for cake making. If you don't have one, simply spoon the flour mixture or icing sugar into a fine-mesh sieve. Tap the sieve against your hand to sprinkle the contents into or over other ingredients.

Maple Leaf Icebox Cake

This Canada Day–themed cake is bright and refreshing.
Choose the ripest, reddest strawberries for the perfect flag topping.

What you need

1¾ cups	whipping cream (35%)
1	pkg (275 g) mascarpone cheese, softened
½ cup	granulated sugar
1 tbsp	vanilla
625 g	fresh strawberries, hulled (about 6½ cups)
1 tsp	grated lemon zest
2 tsp	lemon juice
1	pkg (390 g) golden cake, cut crosswise in ½-inch (1 cm) slices

How to make it

Whip ¾ cup of the cream until stiff peaks form. In large bowl, beat together mascarpone cheese, all but 2 tbsp of the sugar and the vanilla until fluffy, about 1 minute. Gently fold in whipped cream.

Dice 4 cups of the strawberries. In separate bowl, stir together diced strawberries, 1 tsp of the remaining sugar, the lemon zest and lemon juice.

Line 9- x 5-inch (2 L) loaf pan with plastic wrap; arrange one-third of the cake in bottom of pan. Spoon half of the mascarpone mixture over cake; top with half of the strawberry mixture. Repeat layers once; arrange remaining cake over top. Cover with plastic wrap, pressing top of cake gently to adhere. Refrigerate for 12 hours. *(Make-ahead: Refrigerate for up to 24 hours.)*

Remove plastic wrap from top of cake; invert onto platter. Peel off remaining plastic wrap.

In bowl, whip remaining cream with remaining sugar; spread whipped cream over cake, smoothing edges. Slice remaining strawberries and arrange in overlapping rows, forming two side bands and maple leaf in centre.

MAKES 8 SERVINGS. PER SERVING: about 547 cal, 8 g pro, 38 g total fat (20 g sat. fat), 44 g carb, 2 g fibre, 132 mg chol, 229 mg sodium, 156 mg potassium. % RDI: 13% calcium, 9% iron, 28% vit A, 73% vit C, 9% folate.

TEST KITCHEN TIP

To make your Canada Day celebrations even more relaxed, assemble the cake the night before your party. This does two things: It saves time and allows the cake to absorb some of the moisture in the filling, helping it hold together and slice cleanly.

Enjoy a slice of
True North pride.

A light, lemony cake is always a welcome guest.

Glazed Lemon Poke Cake

A classic lemon Bundt cake is a must-have recipe for any occasion. This one, with its triple dose of lemon—in the batter, in the syrup and in the glaze—yields ultra-moist results. Dress it up with fresh berries for a special occasion, or serve plain slices as an afternoon treat.

What you need

1 cup	unsalted butter, softened
2 cups	granulated sugar
1 tbsp	grated lemon zest
1 tbsp	lemon juice
4	eggs, separated
3 cups	all-purpose flour
½ tsp	baking soda
½ tsp	salt
1¼ cups	buttermilk

LEMON SYRUP:

¼ cup	granulated sugar
2	strips lemon zest
1 tbsp	lemon juice

LEMON GLAZE:

1¼ cups	icing sugar
2 tbsp	lemon juice
2 tbsp	unsalted butter, melted

MAKES 16 SERVINGS. PER SERVING: about 375 cal, 5 g pro, 15 g total fat (9 g sat. fat), 57 g carb, 1 g fibre, 82 mg chol, 145 mg sodium, 85 mg potassium. % RDI: 4% calcium, 9% iron, 14% vit A, 3% vit C, 25% folate.

How to make it

In bowl, beat butter with sugar until fluffy. Beat in lemon zest and lemon juice. Beat in egg yolks, one at a time.

Whisk together flour, baking soda and salt; stir into butter mixture alternately with buttermilk, making two additions of dry ingredients and one of buttermilk.

Beat egg whites until stiff peaks form. Stir one-third into batter; fold in remaining egg whites just until combined. Pour into greased and floured 10-inch (3 L) Bundt pan, smoothing top.

Bake in 350°F (180°C) oven until cake tester inserted in centre comes out clean, 50 to 55 minutes. Let cool in pan on rack for 10 minutes; turn out onto rack.

LEMON SYRUP: Meanwhile, in small saucepan, bring sugar, ¼ cup water and lemon zest to boil over medium heat, stirring. Boil, without stirring, for 1 minute. Discard lemon zest; stir in lemon juice. Using skewer, poke holes in top of cake almost but not all the way through. Brush syrup all over top; let cool completely.

LEMON GLAZE: In bowl, whisk icing sugar with lemon juice until smooth; whisk in butter to make thick but pourable glaze. Spoon or pour over cake; let stand until set, about 15 minutes. *(Make-ahead: Store in airtight container for up to 2 days.)*

Apple Pecan Bundt Cake With Caramel Sauce

Bundt cakes are deliciously retro, and this one is no exception.
Tender apples, crunchy pecans and sticky caramel sauce make it
a divine dessert for relaxed entertaining.

What you need

¾ cup	butter, softened
1½ cups	granulated sugar
2 tsp	vanilla
3	eggs
1 cup	sour cream
¼ cup	milk
3 cups	all-purpose flour
1½ tsp	each baking powder and baking soda
1 tsp	cinnamon
¼ tsp	salt
3	Golden Delicious apples, peeled, cored and grated
1 cup	chopped pecans

CARAMEL SAUCE:

⅔ cup	granulated sugar
½ cup	butter
2 tsp	lemon juice
5 tbsp	whipping cream (35%)

MAKES 16 SERVINGS. PER SERVING: about 434 cal,
6 g pro, 25 g total fat (12 g sat. fat), 50 g carb, 2 g fibre, 84 mg
chol, 310 mg sodium, 130 mg potassium. % RDI: 5% calcium,
11% iron, 18% vit A, 2% vit C, 20% folate.

How to make it

In large bowl, beat together butter, sugar and vanilla until fluffy. Beat in eggs, one at a time. Beat in sour cream and milk.

Whisk together flour, baking powder, baking soda, cinnamon and salt; stir into butter mixture. Stir in apples and three-quarters of the pecans. Scrape into greased and floured 10-inch (3 L) Bundt pan, smoothing top.

Bake in 325°F (160°C) oven until cake tester inserted in centre comes out clean, 1 hour. Let cool in pan on rack for 10 minutes. Turn out onto rack; let cool completely.

CARAMEL SAUCE: Meanwhile, in saucepan, cook sugar, butter and lemon juice over medium heat, stirring, until sugar is dissolved and butter is melted. Cook, without stirring, until light amber colour, about 5 minutes. Remove from heat; standing back and averting face, stir in cream. Return to heat; cook until slightly thickened, about 1 minute. Pour into large bowl; let cool to lukewarm.

Pour half of the caramel sauce over top of cake; sprinkle with remaining pecans. Serve cake with remaining caramel sauce alongside.

Apple Streusel Coffee Cake

Coffee cake is such a pleasure to eat for breakfast or a sweet snack. This one stays flavourful and moist even when baked the night before serving.

What you need

2¼ cups	all-purpose flour
1 cup	granulated sugar
2½ tsp	baking powder
¼ tsp	cinnamon
¼ tsp	salt
1 cup	milk
2	eggs
½ cup	unsalted butter, melted
½ cup	sour cream
½ tsp	vanilla

APPLE FILLING:

2¾ cups	thinly sliced cored peeled Granny Smith apples
1 tbsp	granulated sugar
1 tbsp	all-purpose flour

CINNAMON STREUSEL:

¾ cup	all-purpose flour
⅓ cup	unsalted butter, melted
¼ cup	each packed brown sugar and granulated sugar
2 tsp	cinnamon

MAKES 9 SERVINGS. PER SERVING: about 510 cal, 7 g pro, 21 g total fat (13 g sat. fat), 75 g carb, 2 g fibre, 94 mg chol, 184 mg sodium, 180 mg potassium. % RDI: 10% calcium, 18% iron, 19% vit A, 2% vit C, 43% folate.

How to make it

CINNAMON STREUSEL: Stir together flour, butter, brown sugar, granulated sugar and cinnamon until in small crumbs; set aside.

APPLE FILLING: Toss together apples, sugar and flour; set aside.

In large bowl, whisk together flour, sugar, baking powder, cinnamon and salt. Whisk together milk, eggs, butter, sour cream and vanilla; stir into flour mixture until smooth. Spread half of the batter in parchment paper–lined 9-inch (2.5 L) square cake pan.

Arrange apple filling over batter. Pour remaining batter over top, spreading evenly to edges of pan. Sprinkle with cinnamon streusel.

Bake in 350°F (180°C) oven until golden and cake tester inserted in centre comes out clean, about 1 hour. Let cool in pan on rack.

Blueberry Coffee Cake

With tender, sweet blueberries in every bite, this cake is terrific in the summer,
when the berries are at their peak ripeness.

What you need

⅓ cup	butter, softened
⅔ cup	packed brown sugar
2	eggs
1 tsp	each grated lemon zest and lemon juice
1½ cups	all-purpose flour
1 tsp	baking powder
½ tsp	baking soda
¼ tsp	salt
½ cup	plain yogurt (see Tip, below)
2 cups	fresh blueberries

TOPPING:

½ cup	all-purpose flour
½ cup	packed brown sugar
¼ tsp	grated nutmeg
¼ cup	butter, melted

MAKES 12 SERVINGS. PER SERVING: about 269 cal, 4 g pro,
10 g total fat (6 g sat. fat), 41 g carb, 1 g fibre, 56 mg chol, 216 mg
sodium, 155 mg potassium. % RDI: 5% calcium, 11% iron, 9% vit A,
5% vit C, 22% folate.

How to make it

TOPPING: In bowl, whisk together flour, brown sugar
and nutmeg; drizzle with butter, tossing until in small
crumbs. Set aside.

In large bowl, beat butter with brown sugar until fluffy;
beat in eggs, lemon zest and lemon juice.

Whisk together flour, baking powder, baking soda and
salt; stir into butter mixture alternately with yogurt,
making two additions of dry ingredients and one of
yogurt. Scrape into parchment paper–lined 9-inch (2.5 L)
square cake pan. Sprinkle with blueberries and topping.

Bake in 350°F (180°C) oven until cake tester inserted
in centre comes out clean, about 50 minutes. Let cool
in pan on rack.

TEST KITCHEN TIP

This recipe calls for yogurt instead of buttermilk or milk in the cake batter. In baking,
it's best to use full-fat yogurt rather than reduced-fat, unless the recipe specifically calls
for the light stuff. Regular or Balkan-style plain yogurt will work equally well.

A sweet welcome home
makes any day brighter.

Cranberry Coffee Cake
With Almond Streusel

Sweet-tart cranberries add something special and festive to this cake. You can omit the almonds in favour of walnuts, pecans or hazelnuts. Or go nut-free by substituting large-flake rolled oats for the almonds and using vanilla instead of the almond extract.

What you need

¾ cup	granulated sugar
½ cup	unsalted butter, softened
2 tsp	each grated lemon zest and lemon juice
2	eggs
¼ tsp	almond extract or vanilla
1¼ cups	all-purpose flour
1¼ tsp	baking powder
1 tsp	baking soda
¼ tsp	salt
⅔ cup	sour cream
1½ cups	fresh or thawed frozen cranberries, chopped and patted dry
2 tsp	icing sugar

ALMOND STREUSEL:

⅓ cup	all-purpose flour
¼ cup	granulated sugar
2 tbsp	unsalted butter, melted
Pinch	each cinnamon and salt
⅓ cup	chopped almonds

MAKES 8 TO 10 SERVINGS. PER EACH OF 10 SERVINGS:
about 320 cal, 5 g pro, 17 g total fat (9 g sat. fat), 39 g carb,
2 g fibre, 74 mg chol, 243 mg sodium, 98 mg potassium.
% RDI: 5% calcium, 9% iron, 13% vit A, 3% vit C, 22% folate.

How to make it

Grease 9-inch (2.5 L) springform pan; line bottom with parchment paper. Set aside.

ALMOND STREUSEL: In bowl, stir together flour, sugar, butter, cinnamon and salt until in small crumbs. Using fingers, mix in almonds until crumbly. Set aside.

In large bowl, beat together sugar, butter, lemon zest and lemon juice until lightened, about 3 minutes. Beat in eggs, one at a time. Beat in almond extract.

Whisk together flour, baking powder, baking soda and salt; stir into butter mixture alternately with sour cream, making three additions of dry ingredients and two of sour cream. Fold in 1 cup of the cranberries. Scrape into prepared pan; sprinkle with remaining cranberries, then almond streusel.

Bake in 375°F (190°C) oven until golden and cake tester inserted in centre comes out clean, about 50 minutes. Run knife around edge of pan; let cool in pan on rack. *(Make-ahead: Cover and store for up to 3 days.)*

To serve, remove side of pan; dust cake with icing sugar.

Nut-Free Carrot Cake
With Cinnamon Cream Cheese Icing

So many carrot cake recipes call for walnuts, making them off-limits for people with nut allergies.
This nut-free version is a wonderful option for school parties, lunches or bake sales.

What you need

3 cups	all-purpose flour
2 tsp	baking powder
2 tsp	cinnamon
½ tsp	salt
3	eggs
¾ cup	packed brown sugar
¾ cup	granulated sugar
⅔ cup	vegetable oil
1 tsp	vanilla
½ cup	unsweetened applesauce
2 cups	grated carrots
1	can (398 mL) crushed pineapple, drained
½ cup	golden raisins

CINNAMON CREAM CHEESE ICING:

⅔	pkg (250 g pkg) cream cheese, softened
⅓ cup	unsalted butter, softened
3 cups	icing sugar
1 tsp	vanilla
¼ tsp	cinnamon

How to make it

In large bowl, whisk together flour, baking powder, cinnamon and salt; set aside.

In separate bowl, beat together eggs, brown sugar and granulated sugar until pale and thickened. Beat in oil and vanilla. Stir in applesauce. Pour over flour mixture and stir just until moistened. Fold in carrots, pineapple and raisins. Spread in parchment paper–lined 13- x 9-inch (3.5 L) cake pan.

Bake in 325°F (160°C) oven until cake tester inserted in centre comes out clean, 50 to 60 minutes. Let cool in pan on rack.

CINNAMON CREAM CHEESE ICING: In bowl, beat cream cheese with butter until fluffy. Beat in icing sugar, vanilla and cinnamon. Spread over cooled cake.
(Make-ahead: Wrap in plastic wrap and refrigerate for up to 2 days or overwrap in foil and freeze for up to 2 weeks.)

MAKES 24 SERVINGS. PER SERVING: about 297 cal,
3 g pro, 12 g total fat (4 g sat. fat), 46 g carb, 1 g fibre,
38 mg chol, 110 mg sodium, 120 mg potassium. % RDI:
3% calcium, 9% iron, 20% vit A, 2% vit C, 17% folate.

Dress up a humble slice with a fancy espresso or cappuccino.

Sour Cream Chocolate Crumb Cake

Many simple snacking cakes are based on fruit, but this little gem is rich, chocolaty and decadent. And it's still a cinch to make.

What you need

½ cup	unsalted butter, softened
½ cup	granulated sugar
1	egg
1	egg yolk
1⅓ cups	all-purpose flour
½ tsp	baking soda
¼ tsp	salt
½ cup	sour cream
85 g	bittersweet chocolate, melted

CRUMB TOPPING:

½ cup	packed brown sugar
¼ cup	granulated sugar
¼ tsp	cinnamon
Pinch	salt
½ cup	unsalted butter, melted and warm
1⅓ cups	all-purpose flour
⅓ cup	ground almonds

MAKES 12 SERVINGS. PER SERVING: about 387 cal, 5 g pro, 21 g total fat (12 g sat. fat), 46 g carb, 2 g fibre, 77 mg chol, 116 mg sodium, 105 mg potassium. % RDI: 4% calcium, 14% iron, 16% vit A, 29% folate.

How to make it

CRUMB TOPPING: In bowl, stir together brown sugar, granulated sugar, cinnamon and salt; stir in butter. Stir in all-purpose flour and ground almonds, using hands to press mixture together into small crumbs. Let cool.

In large bowl, beat butter with sugar until fluffy. Beat in egg and egg yolk.

Whisk together flour, baking soda and salt. Stir into butter mixture alternately with sour cream, making three additions of dry ingredients and two of sour cream. Stir in chocolate.

Spread in parchment paper–lined 8-inch (2 L) square cake pan. Crumble topping evenly over batter. Bake in 350°F (180°C) oven until cake tester inserted in centre comes out clean, 35 to 40 minutes. Let cool in pan on rack.

CHANGE IT UP

Sour Cream Chocolate Chunk Crumb Cake

Substitute ⅓ cup chopped bittersweet chocolate for the melted chocolate.

Apple Pie Cake

Imagine the flavours you love in pie—sweet apples and warm cinnamon—wrapped up in a tender cake that's perfect for afternoon snacking. Serve with coffee or tea.

What you need

2	eggs
2 cups	granulated sugar
1 cup	vegetable oil
1 tsp	vanilla
2 cups	all-purpose flour
2 tsp	cinnamon
½ tsp	baking soda
½ tsp	baking powder
½ tsp	salt
5 cups	cubed (½ inch/1 cm) cored peeled Spartan apples (see Tip, below)

How to make it

In large bowl, beat together eggs, sugar, oil and vanilla. Whisk together flour, cinnamon, baking soda, baking powder and salt; stir into egg mixture to make stiff dough. Fold in apples.

Spread in parchment paper–lined 13- x 9-inch (3.5 L) cake pan. Bake in 350°F (180°C) oven until cake tester inserted in centre comes out with moist crumbs clinging, 45 to 50 minutes. Let cool in pan on rack.

MAKES 16 SERVINGS. PER SERVING: about 305 cal, 3 g pro, 15 g total fat (1 g sat. fat), 43 g carb, 1 g fibre, 23 mg chol, 129 mg sodium, 62 mg potassium. % RDI: 1% calcium, 6% iron, 1% vit A, 2% vit C, 16% folate.

TEST KITCHEN TIP

Spartan apples are a cross between Newtown and McIntosh apples. They have the rich flavour of the McIntosh but hold up well in baking and cooking. They are juicy and crunchy, so they are also perfect for eating out of hand. If you can't find this variety, try Honeycrisp, Empire or Golden Delicious.

Orange Almond Flourless Snacking Cake

This naturally gluten-free cake is so moist and delicious you won't miss the flour.
It keeps for days in an airtight container at room temperature,
so it's perfect for treats or desserts throughout the week.

What you need

6	eggs, separated
1 cup	granulated sugar
2 tsp	grated orange zest
1 tsp	vanilla
Pinch	cinnamon
2 cups	ground almonds
2 tbsp	orange juice
2 tsp	icing sugar

How to make it

Grease 9-inch (2.5 L) springform pan; line bottom with parchment paper. Set aside.

In large bowl and using hand mixer, beat together egg yolks, sugar, orange zest, vanilla and cinnamon until butter-coloured and thick enough to form long ribbons that hold their shape for 2 seconds when beaters are lifted, about 5 minutes. Fold in almonds and orange juice.

In separate bowl, beat egg whites until stiff peaks form. Stir one-quarter into egg yolk mixture until combined. Fold in remaining egg whites until combined. Scrape into prepared pan; smooth top.

Bake in 350°F (180°C) oven until cake pulls away from side of pan and top is golden and firm to the touch, about 35 minutes. Run knife around edge of pan; let cool in pan on rack for 10 minutes.

Transfer cake to rack; let cool completely. Dust with icing sugar. *(Make-ahead: Store in airtight container for up to 5 days.)*

MAKES 10 SERVINGS. PER SERVING: about 235 cal, 8 g pro, 13 g total fat (2 g sat. fat), 25 g carb, 2 g fibre, 110 mg chol, 38 mg sodium, 180 mg potassium. % RDI: 6% calcium, 9% iron, 6% vit A, 3% vit C, 10% folate.

TEST KITCHEN TIP

Many flourless cakes sink a bit in the middle, so don't worry if that happens—it won't affect the taste. And remember to wait until the cake is completely cooled before dusting it with icing sugar. A too-warm cake will dissolve the sugar as soon as it hits the top.

Chocolate Peanut Butter Pudding Cake

Gooey and luscious, this cake is a miracle of simple engineering. And with a
slow cooker variation, it's the ultimate convenient dessert.

What you need

¾ cup	all-purpose flour
⅓ cup	granulated sugar
1 tsp	baking powder
⅓ cup	milk
1	egg, beaten
3 tbsp	natural peanut butter (see Tip, below)
¾ cup	packed brown sugar
¼ cup	cocoa powder
1 cup	boiling water

How to make it

In large bowl, whisk together flour, granulated sugar and
baking powder. Whisk together milk, egg and peanut
butter until smooth; stir into flour mixture. Scrape into
greased 8-inch (2 L) square baking dish.

In heatproof bowl, whisk brown sugar with cocoa
powder; whisk in boiling water until smooth. Pour over
cake; do not stir. Bake in 350°F (180°C) oven until cake is
firm to the touch, about 30 minutes. Let cool in pan on
rack for 10 minutes.

CHANGE IT UP

Slow Cooker Chocolate Peanut Butter Pudding Cake

Scrape batter into greased slow cooker. Pour cocoa
mixture over top; do not stir. Cover and cook on high
until cake is firm to the touch, about 2 hours.

MAKES 4 TO 6 SERVINGS. PER EACH OF 6 SERVINGS:
about 281 cal, 6 g pro, 6 g total fat (1 g sat. fat), 54 g carb,
2 g fibre, 32 mg chol, 81 mg sodium. % RDI: 7% calcium,
16% iron, 2% vit A, 17% folate.

TEST KITCHEN TIP

This recipe calls for natural peanut butter, which is made from peanuts alone.
It gives the cake a rich, deep nutty flavour that's an excellent complement to the
chocolaty sauce. Don't substitute regular peanut butter—it contains added oil,
salt and sugar that would alter the taste and texture of the cake.

Splurge on real vanilla bean ice cream on top.

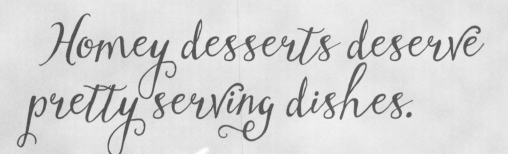

Homey desserts deserve
pretty serving dishes.

Blueberry Pudding Cake

Pudding cakes bake up like magic, with tender cake on top and a warm sauce underneath.
This one, with juicy ripe blueberries, is a comforting one-dish classic.

What you need

3 cups	fresh blueberries (see Tip, below)
⅔ cup	granulated sugar
¼ cup	lemon juice

CAKE TOPPING:

½ cup	butter, softened
¾ cup	granulated sugar
2	eggs
1 tsp	grated lemon zest
½ tsp	vanilla
1¼ cups	all-purpose flour
1½ tsp	baking powder
Pinch	salt
½ cup	milk

MAKES 8 SERVINGS. PER SERVING: about 369 cal,
5 g pro, 13 g total fat (8 g sat. fat), 60 g carb, 2 g fibre,
78 mg chol, 164 mg sodium. % RDI: 5% calcium, 9% iron,
13% vit A, 15% vit C, 22% folate.

How to make it

In greased 8-inch (2 L) square baking dish, toss
blueberries with ⅓ cup of the sugar; set aside.

CAKE TOPPING: In large bowl, beat butter with sugar
until light. Beat in eggs, one at a time. Beat in lemon zest
and vanilla. Whisk together flour, baking powder and salt.
Add to butter mixture alternately with milk, making three
additions of dry ingredients and two of milk. Scrape over
blueberries, smoothing top. Set aside.

In small saucepan, bring ¾ cup water, lemon juice and
remaining sugar to boil; pour over batter. Do not stir.

Bake in 350°F (180°C) oven until bubbly around edges
and cake is firm to the touch, 50 to 55 minutes. Let cool in
pan on rack for 10 minutes. (*Make-ahead: Set aside at room
temperature for up to 4 hours; reheat if desired.*)

TEST KITCHEN TIP

Wild and cultivated blueberries both work well in this dessert. Since the flavour
of the cake relies on the quality of the fruit, save this recipe for summer, when local
blueberries are in season.

Lemon Buttermilk Pudding Cake

As it bakes, this homey confection separates into a layer of light cake on top of a delicious lemon curd. It's lovely on its own, but adding a dollop of whipped cream never hurt anyone.

What you need

3	eggs, separated
¾ cup	granulated sugar
⅓ cup	all-purpose flour
Pinch	salt
1¼ cups	buttermilk
2 tbsp	butter, melted
1 tbsp	grated lemon zest (see Tip, below)
⅓ cup	lemon juice

How to make it

In large bowl, whisk egg yolks with sugar until pale; whisk in flour and salt. Whisk in buttermilk, butter, lemon zest and lemon juice.

Beat egg whites until soft peaks form; fold one-third into buttermilk mixture. Fold in remaining egg whites.

Pour into greased 8-inch (2 L) square baking dish. Place dish in roasting pan; pour enough hot water into roasting pan to come halfway up sides of baking dish.

Bake in 350°F (180°C) oven until top is golden, about 35 minutes. Remove from water; let cool in pan on rack for 30 minutes.

MAKES 4 TO 6 SERVINGS. PER EACH OF 6 SERVINGS:
about 225 cal, 6 g pro, 7 g total fat (4 g sat. fat), 35 g carb,
trace fibre, 107 mg chol, 102 mg sodium, 150 mg potassium.
% RDI: 8% calcium, 4% iron, 8% vit A, 13% vit C, 14% folate.

TEST KITCHEN TIP

When you're grating the zest of a lemon, the rind should be squeaky clean. To remove any wax or pesticide residues, wash the fruit in warm, very lightly soapy water and rinse thoroughly to remove all traces of soap. Pat dry with a towel before zesting.

Berries and Chocolate Cupcakes

Simple ingredients, just one bowl and minimal mixing miraculously add up to the moistest, richest chocolate cupcakes ever. This is a go-to cake batter for any occasion—and it's egg- and dairy-free!

What you need

¼ cup	seedless raspberry jam
¼ cup	blackberry jam
24	blackberries

EASY CHOCOLATE CUPCAKES:

3 cups	all-purpose flour
2 cups	granulated sugar
⅔ cup	cocoa powder
2 tsp	baking soda
½ tsp	salt
2 cups	cold coffee or water
1 cup	vegetable oil
2 tsp	vanilla
3 tbsp	cider vinegar

EASY BUTTER ICING:

1½ cups	butter, softened
6 cups	icing sugar
⅓ cup	whipping cream (35%)
2 tsp	vanilla

MAKES 24 CUPCAKES. PER CUPCAKE: about 456 cal, 2 g pro, 22 g total fat (9 g sat. fat), 65 g carb, 1 g fibre, 35 mg chol, 239 mg sodium, 104 mg potassium. % RDI: 1% calcium, 9% iron, 11% vit A, 2% vit C, 15% folate.

How to make it

EASY CHOCOLATE CUPCAKES: In large bowl, whisk together flour, sugar, cocoa powder, baking soda and salt. Whisk in coffee, oil and vanilla; stir in vinegar. Spoon into 24 paper-lined or greased muffin cups.

Bake in 350°F (180°C) oven until cake tester inserted in centre of several comes out clean, 20 to 22 minutes. Transfer to rack; let cool completely. *(Make-ahead: Store in airtight container for up to 24 hours.)*

EASY BUTTER ICING: In large bowl, beat butter until light; beat in icing sugar, ½ cup at a time. Beat in cream and vanilla until smooth.

Beat raspberry jam and blackberry jam into icing. Spread or pipe over each cupcake; top with blackberry.

Carrot Ginger Cupcakes

A double dose of ginger (ground and crystallized) brings these tender carrot cupcakes to life—and a swirl of cream cheese icing takes them over the top. If you like, garnish each cupcake with more diced crystallized ginger.

What you need

1⅓ cups	all-purpose flour
1 tsp	baking powder
½ tsp	baking soda
½ tsp	ground ginger
¼ tsp	salt
Pinch	cinnamon
2	eggs
⅔ cup	packed brown sugar
½ cup	vegetable oil
¼ tsp	vanilla
1⅓ cups	shredded carrots
⅓ cup	finely diced crystallized ginger

CREAM CHEESE ICING:

¼ cup	cream cheese, softened
¼ cup	unsalted butter, softened
½ tsp	vanilla
1½ cups	icing sugar

MAKES 12 CUPCAKES. PER CUPCAKE: about 323 cal, 3 g pro, 16 g total fat (4 g sat. fat), 44 g carb, 1 g fibre, 46 mg chol, 166 mg sodium, 258 mg potassium. % RDI: 5% calcium, 16% iron, 26% vit A, 5% vit C, 16% folate.

How to make it

In large bowl, whisk together flour, baking powder, baking soda, ground ginger, salt and cinnamon; set aside.

In separate bowl, whisk together eggs, brown sugar, oil and vanilla; stir in carrots and crystallized ginger. Pour over flour mixture; stir until combined. Spoon batter into 12 paper-lined or greased muffin cups.

Bake in 350°F (180°C) oven until cake tester inserted in centre of several comes out clean, 20 to 25 minutes. Transfer to rack; let cool completely.

CREAM CHEESE ICING: In bowl, beat together cream cheese, butter and vanilla until smooth; beat in icing sugar, ½ cup at a time, until smooth. Spread or pipe over each cupcake.

Apple Spice Cupcakes

A cinnamon-infused cream cheese icing graces the tops of these fragrant cupcakes.
The mix of apples and sweet spices makes them an ideal harvest treat.

What you need

½ cup	butter, softened
¾ cup	packed brown sugar
1	egg
½ tsp	vanilla
½ cup	buttermilk
1½ cups	all-purpose flour
1 tsp	baking soda
½ tsp	baking powder
¼ tsp	each cinnamon, ground ginger, nutmeg and salt
Pinch	ground cloves
1 cup	grated cored peeled Honeycrisp apple (see Tip, page 144)

CINNAMON CREAM CHEESE ICING:

⅓ cup	cream cheese, softened
⅓ cup	unsalted butter, softened
½ tsp	cinnamon
½ tsp	vanilla
2 cups	icing sugar

MAKES 12 CUPCAKES. PER CUPCAKE: about 341 cal, 3 g pro, 16 g total fat (10 g sat. fat), 47 g carb, 1 g fibre, 57 mg chol, 260 mg sodium, 84 mg potassium. % RDI: 4% calcium, 7% iron, 15% vit A, 2% vit C, 12% folate.

How to make it

In bowl, beat butter until smooth; beat in brown sugar. Beat in egg and vanilla; stir in buttermilk until combined.

Whisk together flour, baking soda, baking powder, cinnamon, ginger, nutmeg, salt and cloves. Stir into butter mixture along with apple just until combined. Spoon into 12 paper-lined or greased muffin cups.

Bake in 375°F (190°C) oven until cake tester inserted in centre of several comes out clean, 17 to 20 minutes. Transfer to rack; let cool completely.

CINNAMON CREAM CHEESE ICING: Meanwhile, in large bowl, beat cream cheese with butter until smooth; beat in cinnamon and vanilla. Beat in icing sugar, ½ cup at a time, until smooth. Spread or pipe over each cupcake.

Cranberry Almond Squares

Sweet-tart cranberries cooked with a hint of orange make an easy jam-like filling to sandwich between layers of crisp almond pastry. Freshly ground almonds are crunchier than the store-bought ground variety, so whirl whole nuts in a food processor for the nuttiest crust.

What you need

1½ cups	quick-cooking rolled oats (not instant)
1 cup	unsalted roasted whole almonds
⅔ cup	all-purpose flour
½ cup	granulated sugar
½ cup	packed brown sugar
½ tsp	each cinnamon and ground ginger
¼ tsp	salt
⅔ cup	cold unsalted butter, cubed

CRANBERRY FILLING:

5 cups	fresh or frozen cranberries (see Tip, below)
1¼ cups	granulated sugar
1 tsp	grated orange zest
⅓ cup	orange juice

MAKES 16 SQUARES. PER SQUARE: about 299 cal, 4 g pro, 13 g total fat (5 g sat. fat), 44 g carb, 3 g fibre, 20 mg chol, 41 mg sodium, 150 mg potassium. % RDI: 4% calcium, 9% iron, 7% vit A, 8% vit C, 6% folate.

How to make it

CRANBERRY FILLING: In saucepan, bring cranberries, sugar, orange zest and orange juice to boil. Reduce heat to low; cook, stirring occasionally, until cranberries burst and mixture thickens to consistency of jam, about 10 minutes. Let cool for 20 minutes.

Meanwhile, in food processor, pulse together oats, almonds, flour, granulated sugar, brown sugar, cinnamon, ginger and salt until almonds are finely chopped. Add butter; pulse until mixture resembles coarse crumbs.

Press half of the oat mixture evenly into bottom of parchment paper–lined 9-inch (2.5 L) square cake pan. Bake in 350°F (180°C) oven until golden, about 15 minutes. Let cool in pan on rack for 5 minutes.

Spread cranberry filling over crust. Sprinkle with remaining oat mixture, pressing gently to adhere. Bake in 350°F (180°C) oven until topping is golden, about 40 minutes. Let cool completely in pan on rack before cutting into squares.

When fresh cranberries start appearing in stores in the fall, stock up on them for later in the year. Transfer them to a resealable freezer bag and freeze for up to six months.

Buttery, crunchy, chewy squares are perfect any time.

Orange Date Squares

Whether you're enjoying them in the morning, at midday or in the afternoon, these squares are so satisfying. If you prefer a more classic date square, just omit the orange zest.

What you need

2½ cups	large-flake rolled oats
1¼ cups	all-purpose flour
1 cup	packed brown sugar
1 tbsp	grated orange zest
¼ tsp	salt
1 cup	cold butter, cubed
¼ cup	sliced hazelnuts

FILLING:

1	pkg (375 g) pitted dates (see Tip, below)
¾ cup	granulated sugar
2 tbsp	each lemon juice and orange juice

How to make it

FILLING: In saucepan, stir together 2 cups water, dates, sugar, lemon juice and orange juice; let stand for 30 minutes. Bring to boil; reduce heat to medium and boil gently, stirring often, until thickened, about 10 minutes. Let cool.

In large bowl, whisk together oats, flour, brown sugar, orange zest and salt; cut in butter until mixture is in coarse crumbs.

Press half of the oat mixture evenly into bottom of parchment paper–lined 8-inch (2 L) square cake pan; spread date mixture over top.

Toss remaining oat mixture with hazelnuts; sprinkle over date mixture, pressing lightly to adhere.

Bake in 350°F (180°C) oven until light golden, about 45 minutes. Let cool completely in pan on rack before cutting into squares. (*Make-ahead: Cover and refrigerate for up to 3 days or overwrap with heavy-duty foil and freeze for up to 2 weeks.*)

MAKES 24 SQUARES. PER SQUARE: about 206 cal, 3 g pro, 9 g total fat (5 g sat. fat), 30 g carb, 3 g fibre, 20 mg chol, 80 mg sodium. % RDI: 1% calcium, 7% iron, 7% vit A, 2% vit C, 8% folate.

TEST KITCHEN TIP

Pitted dates come in a block and are good for cooking in fillings like the one for these squares. Large, plump whole dates (with the pits still in) are more expensive and better for eating out of hand.

No-Bake Pink Lemonade Cheesecake Squares

These colourful, tangy squares have a delightfully summery taste and a silky, smooth texture. The key to beautiful, even swirls is to patiently spoon alternating dollops of the lemon and raspberry batters over the crust.

What you need

1½ cups	vanilla wafer crumbs (about 50 wafers)
⅓ cup	unsalted butter, melted
1	pkg (7 g) unflavoured gelatin
2	pkg (each 250 g) cream cheese, softened
⅔ cup	sweetened condensed milk (see Tip, below)
⅔ cup	whipping cream (35%)
1 tsp	grated lemon zest
¼ cup	lemon juice
	Yellow paste food colouring (optional)

RASPBERRY PURÉE:

1 cup	frozen raspberries
¼ cup	granulated sugar

MAKES 16 SQUARES. PER SQUARE: about 262 cal, 4 g pro, 20 g total fat (12 g sat. fat), 17 g carb, 1 g fibre, 65 mg chol, 145 mg sodium, 121 mg potassium. % RDI: 7% calcium, 3% iron, 20% vit A, 5% vit C, 5% folate.

How to make it

RASPBERRY PURÉE: In saucepan, bring raspberries, sugar and 1 tbsp water to boil; reduce heat and simmer, stirring often, until thickened, about 5 minutes. Press mixture through fine-mesh sieve to remove seeds; let cool completely.

Meanwhile, stir vanilla wafer crumbs with butter until moistened; press evenly into bottom of parchment paper–lined 9-inch (2.5 L) square cake pan. Refrigerate until firm, about 15 minutes.

In small saucepan, sprinkle gelatin over ¼ cup water; let stand for 5 minutes. Heat over low heat until dissolved, about 2 minutes.

In large bowl, beat cream cheese until smooth; beat in sweetened condensed milk, whipping cream, gelatin mixture and lemon zest. Beat in lemon juice.

Transfer 1¼ cups of the batter to separate bowl; fold in raspberry purée. Tint remaining batter pale yellow with food colouring (if using). Alternately spoon yellow and pink batters over crust. Using knife, swirl batters together. Gently tap pan on countertop a few times to smooth surface; refrigerate until set, about 4 hours.

Cut into squares. *(Make-ahead: Cover and refrigerate for up to 3 days.)*

TEST KITCHEN TIP

You'll have some leftover sweetened condensed milk when you're done with this recipe. Use it up by adding it to your coffee for a decadent, Vietnamese-style beverage.

Blueberry Lime Shortbread Squares

A cookie-crumble crust, rich blueberry filling and buttery pecan topping
make this fresh, fruity take on date squares absolutely irresistible.

What you need

¾ cup	butter, softened
½ cup	granulated sugar
1 tbsp	grated lime zest
¼ tsp	salt
2 cups	all-purpose flour

BLUEBERRY LIME FILLING:

½ cup	granulated sugar
3 tbsp	cornstarch
3 tbsp	lime juice
4 cups	fresh blueberries

PECAN TOPPING:

1 cup	chopped pecans (see Tip, below)
1 tbsp	butter, melted

How to make it

In bowl, beat together butter, sugar, lime zest and salt until fluffy; stir in flour in two additions to form coarse crumbs. Set aside 1 cup; press remainder evenly into bottom of parchment paper–lined 8-inch (2 L) square cake pan.

BLUEBERRY LIME FILLING: Stir together sugar, cornstarch and lime juice; add blueberries and toss to coat. Using potato masher, lightly crush berries just until some liquid is released. Pour over crust.

PECAN TOPPING: Stir together reserved crust mixture, pecans and butter; sprinkle over filling, pressing gently to adhere.

Bake in 375°F (190°C) oven until filling is bubbly and topping is golden, about 1 hour. Let cool completely in pan on rack before cutting into squares.

MAKES 36 SQUARES. PER SQUARE: about 117 cal, 1 g pro, 7 g total fat (3 g sat. fat), 14 g carb, 1 g fibre, 11 mg chol, 46 mg sodium, 35 mg potassium. % RDI: 1% calcium, 4% iron, 4% vit A, 2% vit C, 5% folate.

TEST KITCHEN TIP

Nuts can spoil quickly, so it's best to store them in the freezer to keep them fresh. Buy pecan halves when they're on sale, and use them lavishly in sweets and as a salad garnish.

Date and Prune Squares

Prunes often get a bad rap. But they are wonderful in desserts like this,
especially when partnered with sweet dates, almonds and spices.

What you need

1½ cups	chopped pitted dates (see Tip, page 65)
1½ cups	chopped pitted prunes (see Tip, below)
1 cup	boiling water
¾ tsp	cinnamon
¼ tsp	nutmeg
Pinch	salt
1½ cups	large-flake rolled oats
1¼ cups	all-purpose flour
¾ cup	packed brown sugar
½ tsp	each salt and baking soda
⅔ cup	unsalted butter, softened
2 tbsp	cold water
½ cup	chopped almonds

MAKES 30 SQUARES. PER SQUARE: about 140 cal, 2 g pro,
5 g total fat (3 g sat. fat), 23 g carb, 2 g fibre, 10 mg chol, 60 mg
sodium, 164 mg potassium. % RDI: 2% calcium, 6% iron, 4% vit A,
5% folate.

How to make it

In bowl, combine dates, prunes and boiling water; cover
and let stand for 20 minutes. Stir in cinnamon, nutmeg
and salt; mash with fork until smooth.

In food processor, pulse together oats, flour, brown
sugar, salt and baking soda until oats are chopped, 5 to
10 pulses. Pulse in butter until crumbly; pulse in cold
water until mixture comes together. Press two-thirds
evenly into bottom of parchment paper–lined 13- x 9-inch
(3.5 L) cake pan; spread with date mixture.

Toss remaining oat mixture with almonds; sprinkle over
date mixture, pressing lightly to adhere.

Bake in 350°F (180°C) oven until light golden, 35 to
40 minutes. Let cool completely in pan on rack before
cutting into squares.

TEST KITCHEN TIP

Prunes can stick to the knife when you're chopping them. If it's really bothersome,
spray the knife very lightly with cooking spray before you start—it will deflect all
those sticky bits. Or use greased kitchen shears; they are another excellent time-saving
tool for this task.

Add ice cream and hot fudge for an easy brownie sundae.

The Best Chocolate Toffee Brownies

Food director Annabelle Waugh has been making variations of these brownies for years, and they are now a classic *Canadian Living* recipe. Chopped toffee chocolate bars give them crunch—an idea she picked up from Bonnie Stern when she worked as an intern at her Toronto cooking school.

What you need

115 g	semisweet or other dark chocolate, chopped
28 g	unsweetened chocolate, chopped
½ cup	butter, cubed
1 cup	granulated sugar
2 tsp	vanilla
2	eggs
½ cup	all-purpose flour
Pinch	salt
3	bars (each 39 g) chocolate-covered toffee (such as Skor), chopped

How to make it

In saucepan over medium-low heat, melt together semisweet chocolate, unsweetened chocolate and butter, stirring occasionally; let cool for 10 minutes.

Whisk in sugar and vanilla. Whisk in eggs, one at a time. Stir in flour and salt; fold in chopped chocolate bars. Scrape into parchment paper–lined 8-inch (2 L) square cake pan; smooth top.

Bake in 350°F (180°C) oven until cake tester inserted in centre comes out with a few moist crumbs clinging, about 25 minutes.

Let cool in pan on rack. Cut into bars. *(Make-ahead: Layer between waxed paper in airtight container and refrigerate for up to 3 days or freeze for up to 3 weeks.)*

MAKES 24 BROWNIES. PER BROWNIE: about 137 cal, 1 g pro, 8 g total fat (5 g sat. fat), 17 g carb, 1 g fibre, 28 mg chol, 49 mg sodium, 43 mg potassium. % RDI: 1% calcium, 4% iron, 4% vit A, 3% folate.

TEST KITCHEN TIP

Brownies and other dense, chewy squares really do need to be completely cool before you can cut them cleanly. Chilling them for a few minutes after they cool and wiping your knife clean between cuts with a slightly damp towel will ensure the tidiest edges.

Peanut Butter Swirly Brownies

Gorgeous whorls of sweet peanut butter dress up these chocolaty squares.
They're cakey, decadent and utterly addictive.

What you need

½ cup	smooth peanut butter
½ cup	butter, softened
⅔ cup	granulated sugar
3	eggs
1 tsp	vanilla
140 g	bittersweet chocolate, melted and cooled (see Tip, below)
¾ cup	all-purpose flour
1 tsp	baking powder
Pinch	salt

How to make it

In large bowl, beat together ¼ cup of the peanut butter, the butter and sugar; beat in eggs, one at a time. Beat in vanilla. Beat in chocolate.

Stir in flour, baking powder and salt; spread in parchment paper–lined 8-inch (2 L) square cake pan. By spoonfuls, drop remaining peanut butter over top. Run knife through batter to create swirls; smooth top.

Bake in 350°F (180°C) oven until cake tester inserted in centre comes out with a few moist crumbs clinging, about 20 minutes.

Let cool in pan on rack. Cut into squares.

MAKES 20 BROWNIES. PER BROWNIE: about 173 cal,
4 g pro, 11 g total fat (5 g sat. fat), 15 g carb, 1 g fibre,
40 mg chol, 87 mg sodium, 58 mg potassium. % RDI:
2% calcium, 5% iron, 5% vit A, 8% folate.

TEST KITCHEN TIP

Chocolate can seize and scorch easily if you melt it over direct heat. The easiest and most effective method is to use a double boiler: Place chocolate in a heatproof bowl over a saucepan of hot (not boiling) water. Heat, stirring often, until melted and smooth.

Gluten-Free Super Fudgy Chocolate Brownies

Sure to please chocoholics, these brownies are so rich and fudgy that
there's no need for icing. Plus, they are gluten-free, making them a welcome treat
for people who have celiac disease or are avoiding gluten.

What you need

3	bars (each 100 g) good-quality dark chocolate (70%), chopped
1 cup	unsalted butter, cubed
¼ cup	whipping cream (35%)
4	eggs
1 cup	granulated sugar
¼ cup	cocoa powder, sifted
¼ cup	white rice flour (see Tip, below)
1 tsp	vanilla
1 cup	chopped walnuts

How to make it

In heatproof bowl over saucepan of hot (not boiling) water, melt together chocolate, butter and cream, stirring, until smooth. Let cool slightly.

In large bowl, whisk together eggs, sugar, cocoa powder, rice flour and vanilla; whisk in chocolate mixture and walnuts. Scrape into parchment paper–lined 9-inch (2.5 L) square cake pan.

Bake in 350°F (180°C) oven until puffed and cracked at edges, about 35 minutes. Let cool in pan on rack. Refrigerate until cold, about 1 hour.

Cut into squares, wiping knife between cuts. *(Make-ahead: Cover and refrigerate for up to 1 week.)*

MAKES 25 BROWNIES. PER BROWNIE: about 226 cal,
3 g pro, 17 g total fat (9 g sat. fat), 16 g carb, 2 g fibre,
53 mg chol, 14 mg sodium, 143 mg potassium. % RDI:
2% calcium, 13% iron, 8% vit A, 4% folate.

White rice flour is available in Asian markets, health food stores and some supermarkets. One common brand is Bob's Red Mill, which you can usually find in the health or natural food aisle of larger grocery stores.

Vanilla Bean Amaretti

This four-ingredient cookie couldn't be simpler. The vanilla bean gives it a
lovely hit of flavour without using vanilla extract. Add the scraped vanilla bean pod
to a canister of granulated sugar to perfume it for all of your baking.

What you need

1	vanilla bean
2 cups	natural almonds (see Tip, below)
1½ cups	granulated sugar
3	egg whites

How to make it

Slit vanilla bean lengthwise; using tip of sharp knife, scrape seeds into food processor. (Save vanilla pod for another use.) Add almonds and sugar to food processor; pulse until finely ground but not pasty. Add egg whites; pulse until in thick paste.

Using damp hands, roll by scant 1 tbsp into balls; place, 2 inches (5 cm) apart, on parchment paper–lined rimless baking sheets.

Bake, one sheet at a time, in 375°F (190°C) oven until golden, 15 to 18 minutes. Let cool on pans on racks.

MAKES ABOUT 40 COOKIES. PER COOKIE: about
71 cal, 2 g pro, 4 g total fat (trace sat. fat), 9 g carb,
1 g fibre, 0 mg chol, 4 mg sodium, 55 mg potassium.
% RDI: 2% calcium, 2% iron, 1% folate.

TEST KITCHEN TIP

Natural almonds are whole, raw almonds that have not been roasted or blanched. They still have their papery brown skin, which gives this simple cookie a pretty flecked appearance.

Cookies like these bring back sweet memories.

Peanut Butter and Jelly Cookies

The favourite childhood sandwich is the inspiration for
these tasty treats. Grape jelly is the traditional choice,
but switch it up for another flavour if you prefer.

What you need

½ cup	unsalted butter, softened
½ cup	packed brown sugar
¼ cup	granulated sugar
1	egg
½ tsp	vanilla
⅔ cup	natural peanut butter (see Tip, below)
1½ cups	all-purpose flour
½ tsp	baking soda
¼ tsp	salt
½ cup	grape jelly (approx)

How to make it

In large bowl, beat together butter, brown sugar and granulated sugar until fluffy; beat in egg and vanilla. Beat in peanut butter.

Whisk together flour, baking soda and salt; stir into peanut butter mixture in two additions.

Drop by level 1 tbsp, about 2 inches (5 cm) apart, onto greased or parchment paper–lined rimless baking sheets. Using floured fork, press each to make crisscross pattern and flatten to ½-inch (1 cm) thickness. With back of small spoon, make indentation in centre of each; fill each with about ½ tsp of the jelly.

Bake, one sheet at a time, in 350°F (180°C) oven until bottoms are golden and edges are browned, 10 to 12 minutes. Let cool on pans on racks.

MAKES ABOUT 36 COOKIES. PER COOKIE: about 101 cal, 2 g pro, 5 g total fat (2 g sat. fat), 13 g carb, 1 g fibre, 12 mg chol, 38 mg sodium, 21 mg potassium. % RDI: 1% calcium, 3% iron, 3% vit A, 8% folate.

We call for natural peanut butter in this recipe, but you can use regular peanut butter. Simply reduce the amount of unsalted butter by 2 tbsp and the brown sugar by ¼ cup.

Sweet 'n' Salty Cookies

These confections were inspired by the Compost Cookies made at Momofuku Milk Bar in New York City. They are a little bit crazy but addictive!

What you need

1 cup	unsalted butter
¾ cup	granulated sugar
¾ cup	packed brown sugar
2	eggs
1 tsp	vanilla
2⅓ cups	all-purpose flour
1 tsp	baking soda
¾ tsp	salt
1 cup	chopped candy-coated chocolate pieces, chocolate, caramels or chocolate bar (see Tip, below)
1 cup	crushed or crumbled savoury snacks, such as potato chips, pretzels or Bugles

How to make it

In large bowl, beat together butter, granulated sugar and brown sugar until fluffy. Beat in eggs, one at a time; beat in vanilla.

Whisk together flour, baking soda and salt; stir into butter mixture. Stir in candy and crushed snacks. Drop by 2 tbsp, about 2 inches (5 cm) apart, onto parchment paper–lined rimless baking sheets.

Bake in top and bottom thirds of 350°F (180°C) oven, switching and rotating pans halfway through, until golden, about 12 minutes. Let cool.

MAKES ABOUT 42 COOKIES. PER COOKIE: about 127 cal, 2 g pro, 7 g total fat (4 g sat. fat), 16 g carb, trace fibre, 21 mg chol, 90 mg sodium, 66 mg potassium. % RDI: 1% calcium, 4% iron, 4% vit A, 2% vit C, 8% folate.

TEST KITCHEN TIP

Use whatever goodies you have on hand to make these cookies. Try chopped dark, white or milk chocolate; your favourite chocolate bars; chocolate-covered raisins; peanuts; and savoury snacks, such as potato chips, corn chips and pretzels. They all add up to one glorious indulgence.

Bake up a batch for a
bake sale smash hit.

50¢ ea

Butterscotch Pear Loaf

Sweet swirls of butterscotch sauce elevate this simple pear-laced loaf to sophisticated dessert status. It's especially scrumptious when pears are in season.

What you need

½ cup	unsalted butter, softened
⅓ cup	granulated sugar
⅓ cup	packed brown sugar
2	eggs
1 tsp	vanilla
¾ cup	milk
1¾ cups	all-purpose flour
1½ tsp	baking powder
½ tsp	baking soda
¼ tsp	salt
2 cups	cubed (½ inch/1 cm) cored peeled Bartlett or Bosc pears (see Tip, below)

BUTTERSCOTCH SAUCE:

¾ cup	packed brown sugar
⅓ cup	butter
3 tbsp	whipping cream (35%)

MAKES 1 LOAF, 10 SLICES. PER SLICE: about 390 cal, 5 g pro, 19 g total fat (11 g sat. fat), 52 g carb, 2 g fibre, 84 mg chol, 241 mg sodium, 140 mg potassium. % RDI: 7% calcium, 11% iron, 18% vit A, 2% vit C, 18% folate.

How to make it

BUTTERSCOTCH SAUCE: In saucepan, cook brown sugar and butter over medium heat, stirring, until butter is melted and sugar is dissolved, about 4 minutes. Remove from heat; stir in cream. Let cool to room temperature, about 45 minutes.

Meanwhile, in large bowl, beat together butter, granulated sugar and brown sugar until fluffy; beat in eggs, one at a time. Beat in vanilla just until combined; beat in milk.

Whisk together flour, baking powder, baking soda and salt; stir into egg mixture. Stir in pears and half of the butterscotch sauce. Scrape into parchment paper–lined 9- x 5-inch (2 L) loaf pan. Drop spoonfuls of remaining butterscotch sauce over top; swirl gently using back of spoon or butter knife.

Bake in 350°F (180°C) oven until cake tester inserted in centre comes out clean, about 1 hour. Let cool completely in pan on rack.

Choose Bartlett or Bosc pears that are ripe and fragrant but firm for this sweet loaf. They will be easier to cube and will hold their shape when cooked.

The Ultimate Banana Bread

This is our best version of banana bread, made using the surprising (and mysteriously effective) technique of "marinating" the bananas in a buttermilk and baking soda blend. It delivers on all counts: It's moist, buttery, sweet and chock-full of banana flavour.

What you need

3	ripe bananas, mashed
½ cup	buttermilk
1½ tsp	baking soda
2¼ cups	all-purpose flour
1½ tsp	baking powder
¼ tsp	salt
¾ cup	unsalted butter, softened
1 cup	packed brown sugar
1	egg
1 tsp	vanilla

How to make it

Stir together bananas, buttermilk and baking soda. Let stand for 5 minutes.

Meanwhile, whisk together flour, baking powder and salt; set aside.

In large bowl, beat butter with brown sugar until combined; beat in egg, vanilla and banana mixture. Stir in flour mixture until combined; scrape into greased 9- x 5-inch (2 L) loaf pan.

Bake in 350°F (180°C) oven until cake tester inserted in centre comes out clean, 60 to 70 minutes. Let cool in pan on rack for 15 minutes. Turn out onto rack; let cool completely.

CHANGE IT UP

The Ultimate Chocolate Chip Banana Bread

Stir 1 cup semisweet chocolate chips into flour mixture.

The Ultimate Cinnamon Banana Bread

Whisk ½ tsp cinnamon into flour mixture.

MAKES 1 LOAF, 12 TO 16 SLICES. PER EACH OF 16 SLICES: about 220 cal, 3 g pro, 10 g total fat (6 g sat. fat), 32 g carb, 1 g fibre, 35 mg chol, 200 mg sodium, 133 mg potassium. % RDI: 4% calcium, 8% iron, 8% vit A, 2% vit C, 14% folate.

Orange Sunshine Loaf

A sweet, two-ingredient glaze tops this fragrant orange-infused loaf. If you like, garnish it with orange sprinkles for an added touch of sunshine.

What you need

3	eggs
¾ cup	granulated sugar
⅓ cup	vegetable oil
2 tsp	vanilla
1½ cups	all-purpose flour
1 tbsp	grated orange zest
1¾ tsp	baking powder
½ tsp	baking soda
¼ tsp	salt
⅔ cup	Balkan-style plain yogurt
¼ cup	orange juice

GLAZE:

¾ cup	icing sugar
4 tsp	orange juice

How to make it

In bowl, beat eggs with sugar until combined; whisk in oil and vanilla.

Whisk together flour, orange zest, baking powder, baking soda and salt; stir into egg mixture alternately with yogurt, making three additions of dry ingredients and two of yogurt. Stir in orange juice. Scrape into parchment paper–lined 8- x 4-inch (1.5 L) loaf pan.

Bake in 350°F (180°C) oven until cake tester inserted in centre comes out clean, 40 to 45 minutes. Let cool in pan on rack for 10 minutes. Turn out onto rack; let cool completely.

GLAZE: Set loaf on rack over waxed paper–lined baking sheet. Whisk icing sugar with orange juice; pour over loaf, spreading over top and letting drip down sides.

MAKES 1 LOAF, 12 SLICES. PER SLICE: about 222 cal, 4 g pro, 8 g total fat (1 g sat. fat), 34 g carb, 1 g fibre, 49 mg chol, 167 mg sodium, 69 mg potassium. % RDI: 4% calcium, 6% iron, 3% vit A, 5% vit C, 18% folate.

Stripey Chocolate Peanut Butter Loaf

A simple batter-layering technique yields fun results in this quick-bread recipe. Kids will love the way the stripes emerge as the batter settles into the pan. If you want to make a nut-free version, substitute an equal amount of soy nut butter or sunflower seed butter for the peanut butter.

What you need

⅔ cup	unsalted butter, softened
1½ cups	granulated sugar
2	eggs
1 tsp	vanilla
⅔ cup	natural peanut butter (see Tip, page 52)
2 cups	all-purpose flour
2 tsp	baking powder
½ tsp	baking soda
¼ tsp	salt
1½ cups	milk
3 tbsp	cocoa powder
½ cup	icing sugar

MAKES 1 LOAF, 12 TO 16 SLICES. PER EACH OF 16 SLICES:
about 296 cal, 6 g pro, 14 g total fat (6 g sat. fat), 38 g carb,
2 g fibre, 45 mg chol, 134 mg sodium, 152 mg potassium. % RDI:
5% calcium, 9% iron, 9% vit A, 20% folate.

How to make it

Line 9- x 5-inch (2 L) loaf pan with parchment paper, leaving 1- to 2-inch (2.5 to 5 cm) collar above rim of pan (see Tip, below). Set aside.

In large bowl, beat butter with granulated sugar until fluffy; beat in eggs and vanilla. Beat in peanut butter. Whisk together flour, baking powder, baking soda and salt; stir into butter mixture. Add milk; stir until smooth. Transfer half of the batter to separate bowl.

Whisk cocoa powder with 3 tbsp water until smooth; fold into one bowl of the batter until combined.

Spoon generous ¼ cup of the chocolate batter into bottom of prepared pan; jiggle pan or gently dab batter with spoon to spread; repeat with ¼ cup of the plain batter. Repeat layers, alternating between the two batters.

Bake in 350°F (180°C) oven until cake tester inserted in centre comes out clean, 75 to 85 minutes. Let cool in pan on rack for 10 minutes. Turn out onto rack.

Whisk icing sugar with 1 tbsp water until smooth; brush all over top of warm loaf. Let cool completely. *(Make-ahead: Wrap in plastic wrap and store for up to 2 days or overwrap in foil and freeze for up to 1 month.)*

TEST KITCHEN TIP

This generous loaf may climb above the rim of the pan as it bakes. That's why you need to line the pan with parchment paper and leave a collar that comes at least 1 inch (2.5 cm) above the rim. That way, the sides of the loaf will stay straight and tall, and won't spill over onto your oven floor.

This loaf adds a ray of sunshine to a rainy afternoon.

Lemon Yogurt Loaf

Fresh as spring sunshine, this lemony loaf is perfect with a cup of tea or coffee any time of day.
The miniature variation is perfect for bake sales and gift giving.

What you need

1½ cups	all-purpose flour
1¾ tsp	baking powder
½ tsp	baking soda
¼ tsp	salt
¾ cup	granulated sugar
1¾ tsp	grated lemon zest (see Tip, below)
⅔ cup	Balkan-style plain yogurt
3	eggs
⅓ cup	vegetable oil

SYRUP:

¾ cup	icing sugar
⅓ cup	lemon juice

How to make it

Whisk together flour, baking powder, baking soda and salt; set aside.

In large bowl and using fingers, rub sugar with lemon zest. Whisk in yogurt and eggs; whisk in oil. Stir in flour mixture in two additions. Scrape into parchment paper–lined 8- x 4-inch (1.5 L) loaf pan.

Bake in 350°F (180°C) oven until cake tester inserted in centre comes out clean, 40 to 45 minutes. Let cool in pan on rack for 5 minutes. Remove from pan; place on small baking sheet.

SYRUP: Whisk icing sugar with lemon juice until dissolved. Brush over top and sides of warm loaf, moving loaf around to absorb excess liquid. Return to rack; let cool.

CHANGE IT UP
Mini Lemon Yogurt Loaves
Spoon batter into two parchment paper–lined 5¾- x 3¼-inch (625 mL) mini-loaf pans; decrease baking time to about 35 minutes.

MAKES 1 LOAF, 12 SLICES. PER SLICE: about 223 cal, 4 g pro, 8 g total fat (1 g sat. fat), 34 g carb, 1 g fibre, 49 mg chol, 168 mg sodium, 71 mg potassium. % RDI: 5% calcium, 6% iron, 2% vit A, 5% vit C, 18% folate.

TEST KITCHEN TIP

It's much easier to zest a lemon that hasn't been cut or juiced, so always start by grating the zest even if you don't need it until later in the recipe.

Pumpkin Chocolate Bread

Pumpkin and chocolate may not sound like an ideal combination, but they are.
Enjoy a slice of this spiced loaf with a cup of good coffee for the ultimate cool-weather treat.

What you need

⅓ cup	butter, softened
¾ cup	granulated sugar
2	eggs
1 cup	canned pumpkin purée (see Tip, below)
1 tsp	grated orange zest
2 cups	all-purpose flour
1 tsp	baking soda
½ tsp	baking powder
½ tsp	cinnamon
¼ tsp	salt
Pinch	ground cloves
170 g	semisweet chocolate, chopped

How to make it

In large bowl, beat butter with sugar until fluffy; beat in eggs, one at a time. Stir in pumpkin and orange zest.

Whisk together flour, baking soda, baking powder, cinnamon, salt and cloves. Stir into pumpkin mixture alternately with ¼ cup water, making three additions of dry ingredients and two of water. Fold in chocolate. Spread in parchment paper–lined 8- x 4-inch (1.5 L) loaf pan.

Bake in 350°F (180°C) oven until cake tester inserted in centre comes out clean, about 1 hour.

Let cool in pan on rack for 10 minutes. Turn out onto rack; let cool completely. (*Make-ahead: Store for up to 3 days or overwrap with heavy-duty foil and freeze in airtight container for up to 1 month.*)

MAKES 1 LOAF, 12 SLICES. PER SLICE: about 262 cal,
4 g pro, 10 g total fat (6 g sat. fat), 40 g carb, 2 g fibre,
45 mg chol, 214 mg sodium. % RDI: 2% calcium, 13% iron,
46% vit A, 2% vit C, 24% folate.

TEST KITCHEN TIP

Pumpkin purée comes in cans near the pie fillings, but it's not the same. It's simply puréed cooked pumpkin, with no added sugar or seasonings. It's not interchangeable with ready-made pumpkin pie filling.

Lemon Pound Cake

This buttery pound cake allows the option of making a large loaf or three mini loaves—
in case you want to serve one right away and save the rest for later.

What you need

½ cup	butter, softened
1 cup	granulated sugar
3	eggs
2 tbsp	grated lemon zest
1 tbsp	lemon juice
1 tsp	vanilla
1½ cups	all-purpose flour
¼ tsp	salt
¼ tsp	each baking soda and baking powder
½ cup	light sour cream

GLAZE:

½ cup	icing sugar
1 tbsp	lemon juice

MAKES 1 LOAF, 10 TO 12 SLICES. PER EACH OF 12 SLICES:
about 237 cal, 4 g pro, 10 g total fat (5 g sat. fat), 34 g carb, 1 g
fibre, 72 mg chol, 180 mg sodium. % RDI: 3% calcium, 6% iron,
10% vit A, 3% vit C, 12% folate.

How to make it

In large bowl, beat butter with sugar until fluffy; beat in eggs, one at a time. Beat in lemon zest, lemon juice and vanilla.

Whisk together flour, salt, baking soda and baking powder; stir into butter mixture alternately with sour cream, making three additions of dry ingredients and two of sour cream. Scrape into greased and floured 9- x 5-inch (2 L) loaf pan.

Bake in 325°F (160°C) oven until cake tester inserted in centre comes out clean, about 1 hour.

Let cool in pan on rack for 10 minutes. Turn out onto rack; let cool completely. (*Make-ahead: Wrap in plastic wrap and store for up to 2 days or overwrap in heavy-duty foil and freeze for up to 1 month.*)

GLAZE: Whisk icing sugar with lemon juice until dissolved; pour over cake, spreading over top and letting drip down sides.

CHANGE IT UP

Mini Lemon Pound Cakes
Spoon batter into three greased and floured 5¾- x 3¼-inch (625 mL) mini-loaf pans; decrease baking time to about 45 minutes.

Chocolate-Glazed Chocolate Chip Muffins

With a velvety chocolate topping, these tiny cakes will be your new favourites.
Enlist the kids' help, since these easy to make muffins are a great way to
introduce them to baking basics.

What you need

½ cup	butter, softened
1 cup	granulated sugar
2	eggs
1 cup	milk
1¾ cups	all-purpose flour
2 tsp	baking powder
¼ tsp	salt
1 cup	semisweet chocolate chips
85 g	semisweet chocolate (see Tip, below), chopped
3 tbsp	whipping cream (35%)

How to make it

In bowl, beat butter with sugar until fluffy. Beat in eggs, one at a time. Gradually stir in milk (mixture may appear curdled).

In large bowl, whisk together flour, baking powder and salt; make well in centre. Pour milk mixture into well and stir just until moistened (mixture will appear separated). Fold in chocolate chips. Spoon into 12 large paper-lined muffin cups.

Bake in 350°F (180°C) oven until tops are firm to the touch, 22 to 25 minutes. Transfer to rack; let cool completely.

In small saucepan over medium-low heat, melt semisweet chocolate with cream until smooth; let cool for 10 minutes. Spread over muffins.

MAKES 12 MUFFINS. PER MUFFIN: about 335 cal, 5 g pro, 17 g total fat (10 g sat. fat), 45 g carb, 2 g fibre, 58 mg chol, 175 mg sodium, 145 mg potassium. % RDI: 6% calcium, 11% iron, 10% vit A, 20% folate.

TEST KITCHEN TIP

Semisweet chocolate has a richer, slightly more bitter flavour than milk chocolate. But if you want to make the glaze even more intensely chocolaty, choose a darker variety that contains at least 70% cocoa.

Who says you can't serve a muffin for dessert?

Warm, peachy muffins make mornings much better.

Almond Crumble Peach Muffins

Nothing sets you up for a good day like a crumble-topped muffin for breakfast.
For extra peach flavour, garnish each muffin with a peach slice before baking.

What you need

2⅓ cups	all-purpose flour
⅓ cup	whole wheat or all-purpose flour
1 tsp	baking soda
Pinch	salt
1 cup	packed brown sugar
1 cup	Balkan-style plain yogurt
½ cup	vegetable oil
2	eggs
1 tsp	vanilla
1 cup	diced pitted peeled firm ripe peaches (see Tip, page 14)

ALMOND CRUMBLE TOPPING:

½ cup	packed brown sugar
½ cup	sliced almonds
½ tsp	cinnamon
4 tsp	vegetable oil

MAKES 12 MUFFINS. PER MUFFIN: about 359 cal,
6 g pro, 15 g total fat (2 g sat. fat), 52 g carb, 2 g fibre,
35 mg chol, 139 mg sodium, 242 mg potassium. % RDI:
7% calcium, 15% iron, 2% vit A, 2% vit C, 26% folate.

How to make it

ALMOND CRUMBLE TOPPING: In bowl, stir together brown sugar, sliced almonds and cinnamon; stir in oil until topping clumps together. Set aside.

In large bowl, whisk together all-purpose flour, whole wheat flour, baking soda and salt. Whisk together brown sugar, yogurt, oil, eggs and vanilla; pour over flour mixture. Sprinkle with peaches; stir just until combined. Spoon into 12 paper-lined or greased muffin cups; sprinkle topping over batter.

Bake in 350°F (180°C) oven until tops are firm to the touch, about 25 minutes.

Let cool in pan on rack for 5 minutes. Transfer to rack; let cool completely. *(Make-ahead: Store in airtight container for up to 24 hours. Or wrap individually and freeze in airtight container for up to 2 weeks.)*

TEST KITCHEN TIP

The trick with muffin and quick-bread batter is to stir the wet and dry ingredients just until they are combined (a few lumps are OK). Then stop—trust us! Overstirring the batter until it's smooth or really well mixed will yield tough, dry muffins. A light touch is always better for these treats.

Crunchy-Top Blueberry Muffins

Blueberry muffins are a time-tested morning indulgence. Crowning them with
a sweet orange-almond topping makes them almost too good to be true.

What you need

2 cups	all-purpose flour
¾ cup	granulated sugar
1 tbsp	baking powder (see Tip, below)
1 tsp	baking soda
½ tsp	salt
½ cup	plain yogurt
¼ cup	vegetable oil
2 tsp	grated orange zest
¼ cup	orange juice
2	eggs
1½ cups	fresh blueberries

TOPPING:

¼ cup	granulated sugar
1 tbsp	grated orange zest
	Sliced almonds (optional)

MAKES 12 MUFFINS. PER MUFFIN: about 214 cal,
4 g pro, 6 g total fat (1 g sat. fat), 37 g carb, 1 g fibre,
32 mg chol, 276 mg sodium. % RDI: 5% calcium, 9% iron,
2% vit A, 8% vit C, 15% folate.

How to make it

In large bowl, whisk together flour, sugar, baking powder,
baking soda and salt; set aside.

Whisk together yogurt, oil, orange zest, orange juice and
eggs; pour over flour mixture. Sprinkle with blueberries;
stir just until dry ingredients are moistened. Spoon into
12 paper-lined or greased muffin cups.

TOPPING: Mix together sugar, orange zest, and almonds
(if using); sprinkle over batter.

Bake in 400°F (200°C) oven until tops are firm to the
touch, about 25 minutes.

Let cool in pan on rack for 5 minutes. Transfer to rack;
let cool completely.

Baking powder is perishable, believe it or not. And old baking powder quickly
loses its leavening power. To check if your baking powder is still OK to use, just
add a spoonful to a small dish of hot water. If it fizzes up, you're good to go.

Seeds add crunch
and great nutrition.

Cranberry Seed Muffins

Packed full of healthy ingredients, these muffins make a powerhouse of a breakfast.
They're also excellent tucked into your bag for an energy-boosting snack.

What you need

1¾ cups	all-purpose flour
¾ cup	whole wheat flour
½ cup	oat or wheat bran
1½ tsp	baking powder
½ tsp	each baking soda and salt
⅓ cup	unsalted sunflower seeds
⅓ cup	hulled pumpkin seeds (pepitas)
¾ cup	granulated sugar
¼ cup	packed brown sugar
2 tsp	grated orange zest
2	eggs
1⅓ cups	buttermilk
½ cup	unsalted butter, melted and cooled
2 cups	thawed frozen cranberries (see Tip, page 62)

TOPPING:

3 tbsp	oat bran
3 tbsp	each unsalted sunflower seeds and hulled pumpkin seeds (pepitas)

MAKES 12 MUFFINS. PER MUFFIN: about 342 cal,
9 g pro, 16 g total fat (6 g sat. fat), 46 g carb, 4 g fibre,
53 mg chol, 225 mg sodium, 265 mg potassium. % RDI:
8% calcium, 21% iron, 9% vit A, 3% vit C, 30% folate.

How to make it

In large bowl, whisk together all-purpose flour, whole wheat flour, oat bran, baking powder, baking soda and salt; whisk in sunflower and pumpkin seeds.

In separate bowl, whisk together granulated sugar, brown sugar and orange zest; whisk in eggs and buttermilk. Whisk in butter until combined; stir in flour mixture in two additions just until combined. Stir in cranberries. Spoon into 12 paper-lined or greased muffin cups.

TOPPING: Sprinkle oat bran, sunflower seeds and pumpkin seeds over batter.

Bake in 375°F (190°C) oven until cake tester inserted in centre of several comes out clean, about 25 minutes. Let cool in pan on rack.

Milk Chocolate Scones

These not-too-sweet scones are a delicious treat any time of day but make a decadent addition to a brunch menu. Splurge on quality chocolate for the best flavour.

What you need

¾ cup	whipping cream (35%)
2	eggs
1 tsp	vanilla
2½ cups	all-purpose flour
2 tbsp	granulated sugar
4 tsp	baking powder
¼ tsp	salt
⅓ cup	cold unsalted butter, cubed
2	bars (each 100 g) good-quality milk chocolate, chopped
1	egg yolk

How to make it

Whisk together cream, eggs and vanilla; set aside.

In large bowl, whisk together flour, sugar, baking powder and salt. Using pastry blender or two knives, cut in butter until in coarse crumbs with a few larger pieces. Stir in chocolate. Using fork, stir in cream mixture just until dough forms.

Turn out onto lightly floured surface; knead once or twice until dough comes together. Roll out or pat into 9-inch (23 cm) square; cut into nine squares. Halve each square diagonally.

Place, 1 inch (2.5 cm) apart, on parchment paper–lined rimmed baking sheet. Whisk egg yolk with 1 tsp water; brush over scones.

Bake in 450°F (230°C) oven until tops are golden, 11 to 12 minutes. Serve warm.

MAKES 18 SCONES. PER SCONE: about 201 cal, 4 g pro, 11 g total fat (7 g sat. fat), 22 g carb, 1 g fibre, 56 mg chol, 120 mg sodium, 81 mg potassium. % RDI: 6% calcium, 8% iron, 8% vit A, 19% folate.

TEST KITCHEN TIP

Most scone doughs can either be patted out and cut with a knife into rustic-looking triangles or rolled out and cut into fancy shapes using cookie cutters. The chocolate chunks in this one would make the cookie cutter option a bit tricky, so this easy pat-and-cut method is ideal.

Currant and Cream Scones

Using whipping cream in scones gives them a light, fluffy texture and rich, creamy flavour.
A little more on top, with a bit of sugar, adds a shiny finish.

What you need

¾ cup	whipping cream (35%)
2	eggs
1 tbsp	granulated sugar
⅓ cup	dried currants
2½ cups	all-purpose flour
4 tsp	baking powder
¼ tsp	salt
⅓ cup	cold unsalted butter, cubed

TOPPING:

1 tbsp	whipping cream (35%)
1 tbsp	granulated sugar (see Tip, below)

How to make it

In small bowl, whisk together cream, eggs and sugar; stir in currants. Set aside.

In large bowl, whisk together flour, baking powder and salt. Using pastry blender or two knives, cut in butter until in coarse crumbs with a few larger pieces. Using fork, stir in cream mixture just until dough forms.

Turn out onto lightly floured surface; knead once or twice until dough comes together. Pat out to scant ¾-inch (2 cm) thickness. Using 2-inch (5 cm) round cutter, cut out scones, re-patting scraps and cutting once.

TOPPING: Place scones, 1 inch (2.5 cm) apart, on parchment paper–lined rimmed baking sheet. Brush with cream; sprinkle with sugar.

Bake in 450°F (230°C) oven until tops are golden, 11 to 12 minutes. Serve warm.

MAKES ABOUT 20 SCONES. PER SCONE: about 130 cal, 3 g pro, 7 g total fat (4 g sat. fat), 14 g carb, 1 g fibre, 39 mg chol, 100 mg sodium, 40 mg potassium. % RDI: 4% calcium, 6% iron, 7% vit A, 5% vit C, 16% folate.

TEST KITCHEN TIP

For a sparkly, crunchy finish, you can substitute coarse or Demerara sugar for the granulated sugar in the topping. This is an especially pretty option for special occasions.

Cranberry Shortcakes

The sweet-tart cranberry almond compote is tamed by the fluffy richness
of the biscuits. Toast the almonds in a skillet over medium heat, shaking the pan often,
for about 5 minutes, while the cranberry mixture is cooking.

What you need

2 cups	fresh or frozen cranberries (see Tip, page 62)
½ cup	granulated sugar
1	strip (about 4 inches/10 cm) orange zest
¼ cup	orange juice
1	stick (3 inches/8 cm) cinnamon
1 cup	whole blanched almonds, toasted and chopped

BISCUITS:

2 cups	all-purpose flour
2 tbsp	granulated sugar
1 tsp	each baking powder and baking soda
¼ tsp	salt
½ cup	cold unsalted butter, cubed
¾ cup	buttermilk

TOPPING:

1 tbsp	buttermilk
1 tbsp	granulated sugar

WHIPPED CREAM:

¾ cup	whipping cream (35%)
1 tbsp	granulated sugar

MAKES 10 SERVINGS. PER SERVING: about 396 cal,
7 g pro, 23 g total fat (11 g sat. fat), 42 g carb, 3 g fibre,
49 mg chol, 244 mg sodium, 209 mg potassium. % RDI:
9% calcium, 13% iron, 15% vit A, 7% vit C, 26% folate.

How to make it

In saucepan over medium-high heat, bring cranberries, sugar, orange zest, orange juice, cinnamon stick and ¾ cup water to boil. Reduce heat to medium; simmer, stirring occasionally, until mixture is slightly thickened and cranberries pop, about 15 minutes. Stir in almonds. Transfer to bowl; let cool. Discard cinnamon stick and orange zest.

BISCUITS: Meanwhile, in large bowl, whisk together flour, sugar, baking powder, baking soda and salt. Using pastry blender or two knives, cut in butter until in coarse crumbs. Drizzle in buttermilk; toss with fork until combined. Turn out onto lightly floured surface. Knead just until dough comes together, eight to 10 times. Pat or roll out to ¾-inch (2 cm) thickness.

Using 2½-inch (6 cm) round cutter, cut out biscuits, rerolling scraps and cutting once. Arrange biscuits on parchment paper–lined rimmed baking sheet.

TOPPING: Brush tops with buttermilk; sprinkle with sugar. Bake in 400°F (200°C) oven until puffed and golden, 8 to 10 minutes.

WHIPPED CREAM: Meanwhile, whip cream with sugar. Slice biscuits horizontally in half; sandwich compote and whipped cream between halves.

Ginger Shortcakes
With Oven-Roasted Plums

Crystallized ginger is wonderful with tangy-sweet roasted plums;
look for it in the baking aisle of the supermarket. The shortcakes are so tasty
you'll want to eat them by themselves!

What you need

675 g	firm ripe prune or purple plums (see Tip, below), pitted and quartered
⅓ cup	granulated sugar
2 tsp	lemon juice
⅔ cup	whipping cream (35%)

GINGER SHORTCAKES:

2¼ cups	all-purpose flour
¼ cup	granulated sugar
2 tbsp	finely chopped crystallized ginger
1 tbsp	baking powder
½ tsp	salt
¼ tsp	ground ginger
½ cup	cold butter, cubed
1 cup	milk
1 tbsp	coarse sugar

MAKES 6 SERVINGS. PER SERVING: about 574 cal, 8 g pro,
27 g total fat (16 g sat. fat), 79 g carb, 3 g fibre, 78 mg chol,
480 mg sodium, 427 mg potassium. % RDI: 14% calcium,
24% iron, 28% vit A, 15% vit C, 45% folate.

How to make it

In greased 13- x 9-inch (3 L) baking dish, combine plums, ¼ cup of the sugar and lemon juice. Roast in 400°F (200°C) oven until tender, 20 to 25 minutes. Let cool.

GINGER SHORTCAKES: Meanwhile, in large bowl, whisk together flour, granulated sugar, crystallized ginger, baking powder, salt and ground ginger. Using pastry blender or two knives, cut in butter until in coarse crumbs. Drizzle all but 2 tsp of the milk over top; stir with fork to form soft, slightly sticky, ragged dough.

Turn out onto lightly floured surface; knead gently 10 times. Roll out into 8- x 5½-inch (20 x 13 cm) rectangle. Trim off scant ¼ inch (5 mm) to straighten edges. Cut into six squares; place on parchment paper–lined rimmed baking sheet. Brush with remaining milk; sprinkle with coarse sugar. Bake in 425°F (220°C) oven until golden, 15 to 18 minutes. Transfer to rack; let cool.

In bowl, whip cream with remaining sugar. Slice biscuits horizontally in half; sandwich plum mixture and whipped cream between halves.

TEST KITCHEN TIP

Diminutive prune plums are in season in the fall. They're common in Italian cooking, and many people refer to them as Italian prune plums. These deep purple fruits are nice to eat, but they really shine in baking. And, of course, they are excellent when dried, as their name implies.

Blackberry Hazelnut Meringue

Like hazelnut nougat, this meringue is chewier and softer than the one used in a traditional Pavlova. You can make the meringue a couple of days in advance and keep it well wrapped in a dry area. We like the whipped cream sprinkled with extra coarsely chopped skinned hazelnuts.

What you need

1 cup	whipping cream (35%)
2 tsp	liquid honey
1 cup	fresh blackberries

MERINGUE:

1 cup	skinned hazelnuts
¼ cup	cornstarch
6	egg whites
1 cup	granulated sugar

How to make it

MERINGUE: In food processor, pulse hazelnuts with cornstarch until fine. In bowl of stand mixer, beat egg whites until soft peaks form. With mixer running, beat in sugar, 2 tbsp at a time, until stiff peaks form. Fold in hazelnut mixture. Smooth into 9-inch (23 cm) circle, about 2 inches (5 cm) high, on parchment paper–lined rimmed baking sheet.

Bake in 350°F (180°C) oven until dry and just firm to the touch, 45 to 50 minutes. Transfer to rack; let cool completely, about 1 hour.

Whip cream with honey; spoon over meringue. Arrange blackberries over whipped cream.

MAKES 8 SERVINGS. PER SERVING: about 340 cal, 6 g pro, 21 g total fat (7 g sat. fat), 36 g carb, 3 g fibre, 38 mg chol, 50 mg sodium, 199 mg potassium. % RDI: 5% calcium, 5% iron, 12% vit A, 7% vit C, 9% folate.

TEST KITCHEN TIP

The meringue spreads about 1 inch (2.5 cm) all the way around when baking, so ensure your baking sheet is large enough to accommodate it.

Strawberry Cheesecake Turnovers

Crisp on the outside and gooey in the middle, these flaky turnovers are a cinch to make.
In-season local strawberries are the sweetest, so make these treats in early summer.

What you need

1½ cups	quartered hulled fresh strawberries
4 tsp	granulated sugar
2 tsp	cornstarch
1 tsp	lemon juice
Pinch	cinnamon
1	pkg (450 g) frozen butter puff pastry, thawed (see Tip, page 106)
1	egg
1 tbsp	Demerara or granulated sugar

CREAM CHEESE FILLING:

170 g	cream cheese, softened
⅓ cup	icing sugar
½ tsp	vanilla

MAKES 8 TURNOVERS. PER TURNOVER: about 352 cal, 6 g pro, 22 g total fat (11 g sat. fat), 35 g carb, 2 g fibre, 69 mg chol, 250 mg sodium, 84 mg potassium. % RDI: 2% calcium, 15% iron, 15% vit A, 20% vit C, 4% folate.

How to make it

In small saucepan, stir together strawberries, granulated sugar, cornstarch, lemon juice and cinnamon; let stand for 30 minutes.

Stir 3 tbsp water into strawberry mixture; bring to boil over medium heat. Reduce heat and simmer until thickened and strawberries begin to soften, about 2 minutes. Transfer to bowl; let cool.

CREAM CHEESE FILLING: Meanwhile, beat cream cheese, icing sugar and vanilla until smooth. Set aside.

On floured surface, roll out each half of pastry into 12-inch (30 cm) square; cut each into four squares.

Spread cream cheese filling over half of each square, mounding in centre; top with strawberry mixture. Brush pastry edges with water; fold one corner over filling to make triangle. With tines of fork, press edges to seal; pierce top of each in three places for vents. Transfer to parchment paper–lined rimmed baking sheets. Refrigerate for 30 minutes or for up to 12 hours. *(Make-ahead: Layer between waxed paper in airtight container and freeze for up to 2 weeks; bake frozen, adding 3 minutes to baking time.)*

Whisk egg with 1 tsp water; brush over turnovers. Sprinkle with Demerara sugar. Bake, one sheet at a time, in 425°F (220°C) oven until puffed and golden, 15 to 18 minutes. Serve warm or at room temperature.

Summer Orchard Tart

This simple tart has a barely there pastry that allows summer's juiciest orchard fruits to shine.
Serve with a dollop of whipped cream or a splash of Armagnac for a luxurious finish.

What you need

Half	pkg (450 g pkg) frozen butter puff pastry, thawed (see Tip, below)
¼ cup	apricot jam
1 cup	sliced pitted nectarines
1 cup	sliced pitted peaches
1 cup	halved pitted cherries
⅓ cup	sliced pitted plums
1	egg

How to make it

On parchment paper–lined rimless baking sheet, roll out puff pastry into 10-inch (25 cm) square.

Leaving ½-inch (1 cm) border around edges, spread 3 tbsp of the apricot jam over pastry. Arrange nectarines, peaches, cherries and plums over jam. Stir remaining jam with 1 tsp water until smooth; brush over fruit.

Beat egg with 1 tsp water; brush some over pastry border. Fold up border to make lip around edge of square; brush lip with remaining egg mixture.

Bake on bottom rack in 400°F (200°C) oven until pastry is crisp and golden, about 25 minutes. Let cool slightly before serving, or serve at room temperature.

MAKES 8 SERVINGS. PER SERVING: about 184 cal,
4 g pro, 8 g total fat (4 g sat. fat), 25 g carb, 2 g fibre,
34 mg chol, 101 mg sodium, 145 mg potassium. % RDI:
1% calcium, 6% iron, 6% vit A, 7% vit C, 4% folate.

TEST KITCHEN TIP

Look for butter puff pastry in the freezer section of your grocery store.
It tastes better than puff pastry made with shortening. Thaw the pastry in the
refrigerator overnight.

Cherry and Ricotta Turnovers

Fresh sour cherries are one of the pleasures of the harvest. These flaky turnovers, with a tart cherry and rich ricotta filling, are a welcome addition to any table.

What you need

1	pkg (450 g) frozen butter puff pastry, thawed (see Tip, page 106)
1	egg
2 tsp	maple syrup
2 tbsp	icing sugar

SOUR CHERRY FILLING:

2 cups	fresh sour cherries, pitted
⅓ cup	granulated sugar
1 tsp	lemon juice
1 tbsp	all-purpose flour

RICOTTA FILLING:

¾ cup	ricotta cheese
¼ cup	icing sugar
1 tbsp	grated lemon zest

MAKES 8 TURNOVERS. PER TURNOVER: about 368 cal, 8 g pro, 19 g total fat (10 g sat. fat), 42 g carb, 2 g fibre, 57 mg chol, 207 mg sodium, 105 mg potassium. % RDI: 5% calcium, 11% iron, 14% vit A, 7% vit C, 4% folate.

How to make it

SOUR CHERRY FILLING: In saucepan, bring cherries, sugar and 3 tbsp water to boil. Reduce heat to medium-low; cook, stirring occasionally, until tender, about 15 minutes. Stir in lemon juice. Whisk flour with 1 tbsp water; whisk into cherry mixture and cook until thickened to consistency of jam, about 1 minute. Let cool completely, about 1 hour.

RICOTTA FILLING: Meanwhile, stir together ricotta cheese, icing sugar and lemon zest; set aside.

On floured surface, roll out each half of pastry into 12-inch (30 cm) square; cut each into four squares.

Spread ricotta filling over half of each square, mounding in centre; top with sour cherry filling. Brush pastry edges with water; fold one corner over filling to make triangle. With tines of fork, press edges to seal; pierce top of each in three places for vents. Transfer to parchment paper–lined rimmed baking sheets. Refrigerate for 30 minutes or for up to 12 hours.

Whisk egg with 1 tsp water; brush over turnovers. Brush with maple syrup. Bake, one sheet at a time, in 425°F (220°C) oven until puffed and golden, about 15 minutes. Let cool for 5 minutes. Dust with icing sugar. Serve warm or at room temperature.

TEST KITCHEN TIP For an extra layer of crunch, sprinkle ¼ cup chopped hazelnuts or sliced almonds onto the turnovers before baking.

Peaches and Cream Bread Pudding

Tender, sweet peaches bring a delicious twist to this classic comfort dessert.
Serve warm, with softly whipped cream or vanilla ice cream, if desired.

What you need

8	thick (¾-inch/2 cm) slices day-old French bread
3 tbsp	butter, softened
3 cups	thawed frozen sliced peaches, halved crosswise (see Tip, below)
2 cups	milk
⅔ cup	granulated sugar
½ cup	10% cream
3	eggs
1 tbsp	vanilla
1 tbsp	icing sugar

How to make it

Spread both sides of each bread slice with butter; tear into bite-size pieces. Toss with peaches; arrange in greased 8-inch (2 L) square baking dish.

Whisk together milk, sugar, cream, eggs and vanilla until smooth; pour over bread mixture, gently pressing to soak. Let stand for 5 minutes.

Bake in 350°F (180°C) oven until golden and puffed, and knife inserted in centre comes out clean, 50 to 60 minutes.

Let cool in pan on rack for 10 minutes before serving. Dust with icing sugar.

MAKES 4 TO 6 SERVINGS. PER EACH OF 6 SERVINGS:
about 427 cal, 12 g pro, 13 g total fat (7 g sat. fat), 65 g carb,
3 g fibre, 122 mg chol, 445 mg sodium, 405 mg potassium.
% RDI: 17% calcium, 15% iron, 17% vit A, 5% vit C, 25% folate.

TEST KITCHEN TIP

This pudding is even more spectacular when made with juicy, in-season peaches.
Simply substitute an equal amount of fresh peaches for the frozen.

Peaches give
bread pudding
a fresh twist.

Banana Chocolate Chunk Bread Pudding

Chocolate and bananas are tasty partners, and they update this old-fashioned treat.
Day-old bread is best for creating a not-too-spongy texture.

What you need

8	thick (¾-inch/2 cm) slices day-old French bread
3 tbsp	butter, softened
2 cups	2% or homogenized milk (3.25%)
⅔ cup	granulated sugar
½ cup	10% cream
3	eggs
1	banana, chopped
85 g	bittersweet chocolate, chopped

How to make it

Trim crusts off bread; spread both sides of each bread slice with butter. Cut into pieces; arrange in greased 8-inch (2 L) square baking dish.

Whisk together milk, sugar, cream and eggs until smooth; stir in banana. Pour over bread, gently pressing to soak; let stand for 5 minutes. Sprinkle with chocolate.

Bake in 350°F (180°C) oven until golden and puffed, and knife inserted in centre comes out clean, 40 to 45 minutes.

Let cool in pan on rack for 20 minutes before serving.

MAKES 4 TO 6 SERVINGS. PER EACH OF 6 SERVINGS:
about 455 cal, 12 g pro, 19 g total fat (10 g sat. fat), 62 g carb,
3 g fibre, 121 mg chol, 380 mg sodium, 301 mg potassium.
% RDI: 16% calcium, 15% iron, 14% vit A, 2% vit C, 22% folate.

TEST KITCHEN TIP

This pudding is even more incredible topped with chocolate sauce. Chop 170 g dark chocolate; place in heatproof bowl. In saucepan, bring 1 cup whipping cream (35%) and 2 tbsp corn syrup to boil; pour over chocolate and let stand for 1 minute. Whisk until smooth; stir in 1 tsp vanilla and a pinch of sea salt. *(Make-ahead: Store in airtight container for up to 5 days. Rewarm over medium-low heat or in microwave.)* This recipe makes enough for this pudding, plus leftovers.

Baked Rum Raisin Rice Pudding

Baked rice pudding tends to be firmer than the stove-top variety, and here its custard top adds luxurious richness. The rum gives it a sophisticated edge, but you can leave it out if you like.

What you need

½ cup	sultana raisins
3 tbsp	amber rum or boiling water
1½ cups	2% or homogenized milk (3.25%)
½ cup	whipping cream (35%)
2	egg yolks
1	egg
½ cup	granulated sugar
Pinch	each salt and nutmeg
2 cups	cooked short- or medium-grain rice (1 cup uncooked), see Tip, below

How to make it

Soak raisins in rum for 1 hour or for up to 24 hours.

In large bowl, whisk together milk, cream, egg yolks, egg, sugar, salt and nutmeg; stir in rice and raisin mixture. Pour into greased 8-inch (2 L) square baking dish. Place dish in roasting pan; pour enough hot water into roasting pan to come halfway up sides of baking dish.

Bake in 325°F (160°C) oven until top is firm and golden, about 1 hour. Remove from water; let cool in pan on rack for 15 minutes before serving.

MAKES 4 TO 6 SERVINGS. PER EACH OF 6 SERVINGS:
about 321 cal, 6 g pro, 11 g total fat (6 g sat. fat), 49 g carb,
1 g fibre, 129 mg chol, 46 mg sodium, 233 mg potassium.
% RDI: 9% calcium, 5% iron, 13% vit A, 8% folate.

TEST KITCHEN TIP

A rice cooker makes preparing the rice for this pudding so simple: You just combine the water and rice, and let the machine do the rest. If you don't have a rice cooker, you can also make the rice on the stove top. Just follow the package directions regarding the amount of water and cooking time.

Tropical accents dress up silky tapioca pudding.

Tapioca With Toasted Coconut

A sprinkle of golden coconut on top of this tapioca gives a touch of luxury to an otherwise humble pudding. Add a wedge of pineapple for a fresh, sweet-tart garnish.

What you need

¾ cup	sweetened shredded coconut
4 cups	5% cream
4	strips orange zest
3	whole cloves or allspice berries
2	eggs
⅓ cup	granulated sugar
Pinch	salt
⅓ cup	small pearl tapioca

How to make it

On rimmed baking sheet, toast coconut in 350°F (180°C) oven, stirring occasionally, until golden, about 5 minutes. Set aside.

In saucepan, heat together cream, orange zest and cloves over medium-high heat until tiny bubbles form around edge. Remove from heat; cover and let stand for 30 minutes. Discard orange zest and cloves.

In large bowl, whisk together eggs, sugar and salt; stir in tapioca. Gradually whisk in cream mixture.

Return to saucepan over medium-low heat; simmer, stirring constantly, until thick enough to coat back of spoon and tapioca is puffed and translucent, about 20 minutes.

Scrape into bowl; place plastic wrap directly on surface. Let cool for 30 minutes; refrigerate until cold, about 2 hours. *(Make-ahead: Cover and refrigerate for up to 24 hours.)*

Serve sprinkled with toasted coconut.

MAKES 4 TO 6 SERVINGS. PER EACH OF 6 SERVINGS:
about 313 cal, 7 g pro, 14 g total fat (9 g sat. fat), 35 g carb, 1 g fibre, 115 mg chol, 188 mg sodium, 61 mg potassium. % RDI: 22% calcium, 4% iron, 2% vit A, 4% folate.

TEST KITCHEN TIP

Old-fashioned puddings like this one are easy to make, but they do require you to be hands-on. Be sure to stir continually as the tapioca cooks to prevent the custard from scorching.

Caramel Pudding

This caramel pudding has a taste that's out of this world.
Serve in small cups, with a dollop of whipped cream for a pretty garnish.

What you need

⅔ cup	granulated sugar
½ cup	whipping cream (35%)
¼ cup	unsalted butter, softened
2 cups	homogenized milk (3.25%)
2 tbsp	cornstarch
¼ tsp	salt
2	egg yolks

How to make it

In deep saucepan, stir sugar with ¼ cup water; bring to boil. Reduce heat to medium; boil, without stirring, until amber colour, about 6 minutes. Remove from heat. Averting face and holding pan at arm's length, whisk in cream and butter until smooth, about 2 minutes.

Meanwhile, whisk together milk, cornstarch and salt; whisk into caramel mixture until smooth. Cook over medium heat, whisking frequently, until steaming.

In bowl, whisk egg yolks; drizzle in about 1 cup of the caramel mixture, whisking constantly. Whisk back into pan. Cook (do not boil) over medium heat, whisking constantly, until thickened, about 6 minutes. Strain through fine sieve into clean bowl.

Spoon into small dessert dishes or cups. Place plastic wrap directly on surface. Refrigerate until chilled, about 4 hours. *(Make-ahead: Refrigerate for up to 24 hours.)*

MAKES 6 SERVINGS. PER SERVING: about 286 cal, 4 g pro, 19 g total fat (11 g sat. fat), 29 g carb, 0 g fibre, 118 mg chol, 44 mg sodium, 140 mg potassium. % RDI: 10% calcium, 19% vit A, 3% folate.

TEST KITCHEN TIP

Placing plastic wrap on the surface of the pudding keeps it from developing a skin as it cools. If you like the skin (some people do!), leave the pudding uncovered.

Homemade pudding was almost a lost art, until now.

Cardamom Rice Pudding With Ginger Mango Salad

Gobble up this sweet rice pudding as soon as it's ready, because it thickens and loses its creamy consistency quickly. The mango salad on top gives the dish a vibrancy that's hard to beat.

What you need

Half	vanilla bean (see Tip, below)
3 cups	homogenized milk (3.25%)
½ cup	short-grain rice, such as arborio
2 tbsp	granulated sugar
¼ tsp	ground cardamom
Pinch	grated nutmeg

GINGER MANGO SALAD:

¼ cup	granulated sugar
3	slices (½ inch/1 cm thick) fresh ginger
1	mango, peeled, pitted and cut in thin strips
2 tbsp	fresh mint leaves, torn

How to make it

Halve vanilla bean lengthwise; using tip of sharp knife, scrape seeds into saucepan. Add milk and vanilla pod; heat over medium heat just until bubbles form around edge.

Stir in rice, sugar, cardamom and nutmeg; bring to boil. Reduce heat and simmer, stirring often, until rice is tender, mixture is creamy and most of the liquid is absorbed, about 30 minutes. Discard vanilla pod.

GINGER MANGO SALAD: Meanwhile, in small saucepan over medium heat, combine ¾ cup water, sugar and ginger; bring to boil. Reduce heat and simmer until sugar is dissolved, about 5 minutes. Remove from heat; let cool slightly. Stir in mango.

Just before serving, drain mango, discarding ginger and syrup; stir in mint. Serve over rice pudding.

MAKES 4 SERVINGS. PER SERVING: about 289 cal, 8 g pro, 6 g total fat (4 g sat. fat), 50 g carb, 2 g fibre, 18 mg chol, 77 mg sodium, 391 mg potassium. % RDI: 20% calcium, 4% iron, 10% vit A, 25% vit C, 9% folate.

TEST KITCHEN TIP

The vanilla bean we call for in the ingredient list should be halved crosswise; if you cut it lengthwise, the moist seeds of the unused portion will quickly dry out and lose their flavour. Wrap the remaining half tightly in plastic wrap and store it in a resealable bag with all the air pressed out. Or return it to the sealed bottle the bean came in.

Chocolate Caramel Layered Pudding

Layers of silky milk chocolate and caramel puddings come together for a luscious flavour explosion. Toffee bits give each spoonful just a hint of crunch.

What you need

½ cup	whipping cream (35%)
¼ cup	toffee bits

CARAMEL PUDDING:

⅓ cup	granulated sugar
¼ cup	whipping cream (35%)
2 tbsp	unsalted butter, softened
1 cup	homogenized milk (3.25%)
1 tbsp	cornstarch
Pinch	salt
1	egg yolk

MILK CHOCOLATE PUDDING:

1 cup	homogenized milk (3.25%)
4 tsp	cornstarch
1 tbsp	granulated sugar
1 tbsp	cocoa powder
Pinch	salt
1	egg yolk
¼ cup	whipping cream (35%)
55 g	milk chocolate, chopped

MAKES 6 SERVINGS. PER SERVING: about 382 cal, 5 g pro, 28 g total fat (16 g sat. fat), 31 g carb, 1 g fibre, 141 mg chol, 89 mg sodium, 219 mg potassium. % RDI: 13% calcium, 4% iron, 25% vit A, 7% folate.

How to make it

CARAMEL PUDDING: In deep saucepan, stir sugar with 2 tbsp water; bring to boil. Reduce heat to medium and boil, without stirring, until amber colour, 4 to 6 minutes. Remove from heat. Averting face and holding pan at arm's length, whisk in cream and butter until smooth, about 1 minute.

Meanwhile, whisk together milk, cornstarch and salt; whisk into caramel mixture until smooth. Cook over medium heat, whisking frequently, until steaming.

In bowl, whisk egg yolk; drizzle in about 1 cup of the caramel mixture, whisking constantly. Whisk back into pan. Cook (do not boil) over medium heat, whisking constantly, until thickened, 4 to 6 minutes. Strain through fine sieve into clean bowl.

MILK CHOCOLATE PUDDING: In saucepan, whisk together milk, cornstarch, sugar, cocoa powder and salt; cook over medium heat just until steaming. In bowl, whisk egg yolk; whisk in half of the hot milk mixture in slow steady stream. Gradually whisk back into pan. Whisk in cream and chocolate; cook over medium heat, whisking constantly, until bubbly and thickened, 4 to 6 minutes. Strain through fine sieve into clean bowl.

In small glass dessert dishes, alternately layer milk chocolate and caramel puddings, making two layers of chocolate and one of caramel. Place plastic wrap directly on surface. Refrigerate until chilled, about 4 hours. (*Make-ahead: Refrigerate for up to 24 hours.*)

Whip cream; spoon over pudding. Sprinkle with toffee bits.

Vanilla Bean Pudding

A double dose of vanilla—from both bean and extract—lends a beautiful fragrance and taste to this pudding. Use pure vanilla instead of imitation for a true, clean flavour.

What you need

½ cup	granulated sugar
2 tbsp	cornstarch
Half	vanilla bean (see Tip, page 119)
2¼ cups	homogenized milk (3.25%)
2	eggs
1 tbsp	unsalted butter, cubed
1 tsp	vanilla
Pinch	salt

MAKES 6 SERVINGS. PER SERVING: about 175 cal, 5 g pro, 7 g total fat (3 g sat. fat), 24 g carb, 0 g fibre, 75 mg chol, 58 mg sodium, 153 mg potassium. % RDI: 10% calcium, 2% iron, 7% vit A, 6% folate.

How to make it

In saucepan, whisk sugar with cornstarch. Halve vanilla bean lengthwise; using tip of sharp knife, scrape seeds into pan. Add vanilla pod. Whisk in milk; cook over medium heat, stirring, just until steaming. Remove vanilla pod.

In bowl, whisk eggs; whisk in half of the hot milk mixture in slow steady stream. Gradually whisk back into pan; cook over medium heat, whisking constantly, until bubbly and thickened, 5 to 8 minutes. Whisk in butter, vanilla and salt.

Strain through fine sieve into clean bowl; place plastic wrap directly on surface. Refrigerate until chilled, about 4 hours. *(Make-ahead: Refrigerate for up to 2 days; whisk before serving.)*

CHANGE IT UP

Dark Chocolate Pudding
Omit vanilla bean. Whisk ⅓ cup cocoa powder with sugar and cornstarch. Add 55 g dark chocolate, chopped, with butter; whisk until melted and smooth.

Chai Spice Pudding
Omit vanilla bean. Decrease vanilla to ½ tsp. Add 4 whole cloves, 2 cardamom pods and 1 cinnamon stick with milk. Discard whole spices before whisking in butter, vanilla and salt.

Pumpkin Amaretti Mousse

An easy no-cook method employs a food processor to whip pumpkin, yogurt and cream into a silky-smooth (and foolproof!) treat. Crumbled amaretti cookies are a quick, crunchy topping.

What you need

1 cup	canned pumpkin purée (see Tip, page 88)
1 cup	plain 10% Mediterranean-style yogurt (such as Liberté Méditerranée Plain 10%)
½ cup	granulated sugar
1 tsp	cinnamon
½ tsp	ground ginger
½ tsp	vanilla
Pinch	each ground cloves and nutmeg
1⅓ cups	whipping cream (35%)
2	amaretti cookies, finely chopped (about ¼ cup)

How to make it

In food processor, blend together pumpkin, yogurt, all but 1 tbsp of the sugar, the cinnamon, ginger, vanilla, cloves and nutmeg until smooth; scrape into large bowl. Set aside.

Whip 1 cup of the cream with remaining sugar until stiff peaks form; fold into pumpkin mixture. Spoon into eight small cups or ramekins; cover with plastic wrap and refrigerate until set, about 2 hours. *(Make-ahead: Refrigerate for up to 2 days.)*

Whip remaining cream until stiff peaks form. Spoon over mousse; sprinkle with amaretti crumbs.

MAKES 8 SERVINGS. PER SERVING: about 239 cal, 3 g pro, 17 g total fat (11 g sat. fat), 20 g carb, 1 g fibre, 63 mg chol, 39 mg sodium, 165 mg potassium. % RDI: 8% calcium, 4% iron, 56% vit A, 2% vit C, 2% folate.

This no-cook mousse is so good, you'll never have leftovers.

Silky Mango Yogurt Mousse

This mousse is lightened up a bit with yogurt, which also gives it
a delightful tangy edge. Making it a day before serving ensures the flavours
really meld and the mousse is chilled perfectly.

What you need

2	ripe mangoes (see Tip, below)
1	pkg (7 g) unflavoured gelatin
2 tbsp	lemon juice
⅓ cup	granulated sugar
½ tsp	vanilla
1 cup	2% plain yogurt
1 cup	whipping cream (35%)

MANGO GARNISH:

1	ripe mango
2 tbsp	granulated sugar
1 tbsp	minced fresh mint
1 tbsp	dark rum
1 tsp	grated lemon zest
1 tbsp	lemon juice

How to make it

Peel, pit and cube mangoes to make about 3 cups;
set aside.

In small saucepan, sprinkle gelatin over ¼ cup water;
let stand for 5 minutes. Heat over low heat, stirring,
until dissolved.

Meanwhile, in blender or food processor, purée mangoes
with lemon juice; strain through fine sieve into bowl.
Add sugar and vanilla; stir until sugar is dissolved. Stir in
gelatin mixture and yogurt.

Whip cream; fold one-third into mango mixture. Fold in
remaining whipped cream. Spoon into six dessert glasses
or ramekins; cover and refrigerate until set, about 4 hours.
(Make-ahead: Refrigerate for up to 24 hours.)

MANGO GARNISH: Peel, pit and dice mango. Toss
together mango, sugar, mint, rum, lemon zest and lemon
juice. Spoon over mousse.

MAKES 6 SERVINGS. PER SERVING: about 323 cal,
6 g pro, 15 g total fat (9 g sat. fat), 44 g carb, 1 g fibre,
53 g chol, 50 mg sodium. % RDI: 11% calcium, 2% iron,
77% vit A, 78% vit C, 14 % folate.

For desserts like this, you need ripe, sweet mangoes. Look for fruit with a red-tinged peel;
it should yield slightly to pressure from your fingers. The stem end should be fragrant.
If sap is oozing from the stem and the fruit is unbruised, it will have the best flavour.

Luscious Lemon Mousse

This punchy lemon mousse will cleanse the palate and satisfy
sweet cravings at the end of a meal. Garnish with fresh berries, toasted coconut
or crushed ginger cookies for a special finish.

What you need

6	egg yolks
2	eggs
1 cup	granulated sugar
¾ cup	lemon juice
1½ cups	whipping cream (35%)
1 tsp	vanilla

How to make it

In large heatproof bowl, whisk together egg yolks, eggs, sugar and lemon juice. Set bowl over saucepan of simmering water; cook, stirring constantly, until thick enough to mound on spoon and mixture holds its shape when a spoon is drawn through it, 10 to 12 minutes.

Strain through fine-mesh sieve into clean large bowl. Place plastic wrap directly on surface; refrigerate until cold, about 1 hour.

Whip cream with vanilla until fluffy and medium-firm peaks form. Gently stir one-third of the whipped cream into lemon mixture; fold in remaining whipped cream. *(Make-ahead: Cover and refrigerate for up to 24 hours.)*

MAKES 10 SERVINGS. PER SERVING: about 250 cal, 4 g pro, 17 g total fat (9 g sat. fat), 22 g carb, trace fibre, 205 mg chol, 33 mg sodium, 71 mg potassium. % RDI: 4% calcium, 4% iron, 19% vit A, 5% vit C, 11% folate.

Fluffy mousse is a dreamy ending to a big meal.

Silky Chocolate Mousse

Nothing says decadence like a luscious chocolate mousse. The sweet,
creamy flavour of the milk chocolate and the deep, rich taste of the dark
give this mousse the best qualities of both.

What you need

115 g	milk chocolate, chopped
55 g	dark chocolate (70%), chopped
1½ cups	whipping cream (35%)
4	egg yolks
3 tbsp	granulated sugar
Pinch	salt
½ tsp	vanilla

How to make it

In heatproof bowl over saucepan of hot (not boiling) water, melt milk chocolate and dark chocolate, stirring, until smooth. Set aside.

In small saucepan, heat ½ cup of the cream over medium-high heat just until tiny bubbles form around edge of pan.

In separate heatproof bowl, whisk together egg yolks, sugar and salt; slowly whisk in hot cream. Place bowl over saucepan of gently simmering water; cook, stirring, until instant-read thermometer reads 160°F (71°C) and mixture is thick enough to coat back of spoon, about 15 minutes. Remove from heat.

Whisk in melted chocolate and vanilla. Pour into bowl; place plastic wrap directly on surface. Let cool for 15 minutes.

Whip remaining cream; fold one-quarter into chocolate mixture. Fold in remaining whipped cream. Divide among six dessert dishes; cover and refrigerate until set, about 4 hours. *(Make-ahead: Cover and refrigerate for up to 24 hours.)*

CHANGE IT UP

Silky Mocha Mousse

Heat 2 tbsp instant coffee granules with cream.

MAKES 6 SERVINGS. PER SERVING: about 413 cal, 5 g pro, 34 g total fat (20 g sat. fat), 24 g carb, 2 g fibre, 209 mg chol, 43 mg sodium, 201 mg potassium. % RDI: 9% calcium, 14% iron, 27% vit A, 10% folate.

Cranberry Raspberry Mousse

The perfect balance of sweet, tart and creamy, this airy mousse makes
a delightful finish to any harvest dinner. It's the prettiest pink you can imagine.

What you need

2 cups	frozen cranberries (see Tip, page 62)
2 cups	frozen raspberries
1 cup	granulated sugar
1	strip orange zest (see Tip, below)
2 tbsp	orange juice
1	pkg (7 g) unflavoured gelatin
1½ cups	whipping cream (35%)

How to make it

In saucepan, bring cranberries, raspberries, sugar, orange zest, orange juice and 2 tbsp water to boil; reduce heat and simmer until cranberries pop, about 6 minutes. Discard orange zest.

In food processor or blender, purée cranberry mixture until smooth. Press through fine sieve into large bowl.

Meanwhile, in small saucepan, sprinkle gelatin over ½ cup water; let stand until softened, about 5 minutes. Warm over low heat until dissolved, about 1 minute. Stir into cranberry mixture. Place bowl in larger bowl of ice water to chill, stirring frequently, until cold and thickened to consistency of egg whites, about 5 minutes.

Whip cream; whisk one-quarter into cranberry mixture. Fold in remaining whipped cream. Divide among eight dessert dishes; cover and refrigerate until set, about 4 hours. (*Make-ahead: Refrigerate for up to 24 hours.*)

MAKES 8 SERVINGS. PER SERVING: about 270 cal, 2 g pro, 16 g total fat (10 g sat. fat), 31 g carb, 1 g fibre, 57 mg chol, 19 mg sodium, 112 mg potassium. % RDI: 4% calcium, 2% iron, 15% vit A, 15% vit C, 3% folate.

TEST KITCHEN TIP

A very sharp vegetable peeler is an ideal tool for making strips of citrus zest. If your peeler is dull, you can use a sharp paring knife to cut off a strip instead. Just make sure to scrape off any of the bitter white pith before you add the zest to the other ingredients.

Four simple ingredients equal one fabulous dessert.

Hazelnut Chocolate Mousse

No one will believe how easy it is to make this delectable dessert. The hazelnuts on top are optional, but they add a wonderful crunchy contrast to the chocolaty mousse.

What you need

½ cup	hazelnut chocolate spread (such as Nutella)
1 tbsp	unsalted butter, softened
¾ cup	whipping cream (35%)
12	toasted hazelnuts (optional), halved

How to make it

In heatproof bowl over saucepan of hot (not boiling) water, melt chocolate spread with 3 tbsp water, stirring, until smooth; stir in butter. Keep warm.

Whip cream; fold one-third into chocolate mixture. Fold in remaining whipped cream. Divide among four dessert glasses or ramekins; cover and refrigerate until chilled, about 2 hours.

Garnish with hazelnuts (if using).

MAKES 4 SERVINGS. PER SERVING: about 388 cal, 4 g pro, 31 g total fat (14 g sat. fat), 26 g carb, 2 g fibre, 66 mg chol, 32 mg sodium, 229 mg potassium. % RDI: 8% calcium, 7% iron, 20% vit A, 4% folate.

TEST KITCHEN TIP

For a truly decadent finish, omit the hazelnut garnish. Instead, top the mousse with crushed chocolate-covered hazelnut candies (such as Ferrero Rocher). This is an excellent way to use up leftovers after the holidays.

Classic Vanilla Crème Brûlée

Decadent custard desserts are adored by French Canadians (OK, all Canadians). To celebrate this love affair, we've created the ultimate classic crème brûlée. A great trick for getting the perfect glassy, crunchy sugar topping is to combine granulated and brown sugars.

What you need

1	vanilla bean
1 cup	milk
1 cup	whipping cream (35%)
Pinch	salt
5	egg yolks
3 tbsp	granulated sugar

TOPPING:

2 tbsp	granulated sugar
2 tbsp	packed brown sugar

MAKES 6 SERVINGS. PER SERVING: about 265 cal, 5 g pro, 19 g total fat (11 g sat. fat), 18 g carb, 0 g fibre, 224 mg chol, 39 mg sodium, 127 mg potassium. % RDI: 9% calcium, 4% iron, 20% vit A, 11% folate.

How to make it

Halve vanilla bean lengthwise. In saucepan, combine vanilla bean, milk, cream and salt; bring to boil over medium heat. Remove from heat; cover and let stand for 10 minutes. Discard vanilla bean.

In bowl, whisk egg yolks with sugar until pale and thickened, about 2 minutes. Stirring constantly with heatproof spatula, add milk mixture in slow, steady stream. Strain through fine-mesh sieve into clean bowl.

Divide egg mixture among six 6-oz (175 mL) ramekins; arrange ramekins in shallow roasting pan. Pour enough warm water into roasting pan to come halfway up sides of ramekins.

Bake in 350°F (180°C) oven until skin forms on surface, edge is lightly set and custard is still slightly jiggly in centre, 25 to 30 minutes.

Transfer ramekins to rack; let cool. Cover and refrigerate for 4 hours. *(Make-ahead: Refrigerate for up to 24 hours.)*

TOPPING: Mix granulated sugar with brown sugar; sprinkle evenly over tops of custards. Place ramekins on baking sheet; broil, 6 inches (15 cm) from element, watching carefully, until sugar is melted and caramel colour, 2 to 4 minutes. Let cool before serving.

Pumpkin Caramel Custards

Though this recipe requires you to roast a pumpkin or squash to make the purée,
it's a simple process. Sugar pumpkins are firmer and sweeter than those grown for
jack-o'-lanterns; you'll see them in stores in the autumn.

What you need

1 cup	granulated sugar
⅓ cup	cold water

CUSTARD:

1 cup	roasted pumpkin or squash purée (see Tip, below)
1	can (400 mL) coconut milk
⅔ cup	granulated sugar
5	eggs
3	egg yolks
2 tsp	finely grated fresh ginger
½ tsp	ground cardamom
¼ tsp	nutmeg
Pinch	salt

How to make it

In heavy-bottomed saucepan, melt sugar with cold water over medium heat, swirling pan but not stirring, until most of the sugar is golden. Bring to boil and boil until deep amber, about 7 minutes.

Pour caramel into eight 6-oz (175 mL) custard cups or ramekins, swirling to coat bottoms and sides. Place in large roasting pan lined with kitchen towel.

CUSTARD: In saucepan, cook pumpkin purée over medium-high heat, stirring constantly, until no liquid remains, 3 to 4 minutes. Whisk in coconut milk; heat just until simmering. Remove from heat; set aside.

In large bowl, beat together sugar, eggs, egg yolks, ginger, cardamom, nutmeg and salt; gradually stir in pumpkin mixture. Strain through fine sieve. Pour into caramel-lined cups. Pour enough boiling water into roasting pan to come halfway up sides of cups.

Bake in 325°F (160°C) oven until set around edges but still slightly jiggly in centres, 40 to 45 minutes. Transfer cups to rack; let cool to room temperature. Run knife around edge of each custard; invert onto plate.

MAKES 8 SERVINGS. PER SERVING: about 335 cal, 6 g pro, 15 g total fat (11 g sat. fat), 46 g carb, 1 g fibre, 193 mg chol, 48 mg sodium, 219 mg potassium. % RDI: 4% calcium, 19% iron, 68% vit A, 3% vit C, 16% folate.

TEST KITCHEN TIP

To make the purée, halve and seed sugar pumpkin or butternut squash. Prick all over with fork. Roast, cut side down, on rack on foil-lined rimmed baking sheet in 350°F (180°C) oven until flesh is browned and tender, 60 to 75 minutes. Let cool. Scoop out flesh; purée in food processor. *(Make-ahead: Refrigerate in airtight container for up to 2 days or freeze for up to 3 weeks.)* A 900 g sugar pumpkin yields about 1¾ cups purée. A 900 g butternut squash yields about 2½ cups purée.

Buttermilk Panna Cotta With Macerated Strawberries

This classic dessert has a wonderful sweet-tangy balance, thanks to the addition of buttermilk. It takes only 15 minutes of hands-on time to prepare, leaving you plenty of breathing room to make other dishes for dinner.

What you need

2	pkg (each 7 g) unflavoured gelatin
1½ cups	whipping cream (35%)
½ cup	granulated sugar
1 tbsp	vanilla
2½ cups	buttermilk

MACERATED STRAWBERRIES:

1	pkg (454 g) fresh strawberries, hulled and thinly sliced
2 tbsp	granulated sugar
Pinch	pepper

How to make it

In small saucepan, sprinkle gelatin over ⅓ cup of the cream; let stand for 5 minutes. Heat over medium-low heat, stirring often, until gelatin is dissolved, about 3 minutes.

In separate saucepan, heat together remaining cream, sugar and vanilla, stirring occasionally, until sugar is dissolved, about 5 minutes. Stir in gelatin mixture. Pour into large glass measure; stir in buttermilk. Divide among eight 6-oz (175 mL) ramekins. Cover with plastic wrap and refrigerate until set, about 3 hours. *(Make-ahead: Refrigerate for up to 24 hours.)*

MACERATED STRAWBERRIES: Meanwhile, toss together strawberries, sugar and pepper; let stand until syrupy, about 1 hour.

Invert panna cotta onto eight dessert plates; top with strawberry mixture.

MAKES 8 SERVINGS. PER SERVING: about 273 cal, 6 g pro, 17 g total fat (11 g sat. fat), 25 g carb, 1 g fibre, 63 mg chol, 86 mg sodium, 253 mg potassium. % RDI: 13% calcium, 2% iron, 16% vit A, 52% vit C, 8% folate.

Berries With Sabayon

A classic culinary sauce, warm sabayon elevates an ordinary combination of fruit to a special occasion dessert. This makes a simple, elegant end to an entertaining meal.

What you need

2 cups	fresh strawberries, hulled and quartered
1 cup	fresh raspberries
¼ cup	slivered almonds (optional), lightly toasted

SABAYON:

4	egg yolks
½ cup	dry Marsala or fruity white wine (such as Riesling)
¼ cup	granulated sugar

How to make it

Gently toss strawberries with raspberries to combine. Divide among six dessert dishes. Set aside.

SABAYON: In large heatproof bowl over saucepan of gently simmering (not boiling) water, whisk together egg yolks, Marsala and sugar until thick enough to mound softly on spoon, 5 to 7 minutes.

Spoon sabayon over fruit. Sprinkle with almonds (if using).

MAKES 6 SERVINGS. PER SERVING: about 126 cal, 3 g pro, 4 g total fat (1 g sat. fat), 17 g carb, 3 g fibre, 136 mg chol, 7 mg sodium, 146 mg potassium. % RDI: 3% calcium, 6% iron, 6% vit A, 63% vit C, 16% folate.

TEST KITCHEN TIP

When you're setting up a bain-marie (also known as a double boiler) to make custard or melt chocolate, make sure the heatproof bowl fits securely over the saucepan to prevent steam from escaping. This is especially important when melting chocolate, because exposure to excess moisture can cause chocolate to seize and clump.

Mini No-Bake Cheesecakes

These mini-cheesecakes were inspired by the ones served at Charcut Roast House, a popular Calgary eatery. In season, try substituting chopped fresh fruit or whole berries for the preserves.

What you need

Half	vanilla bean (see Tip, page 119)
¾ cup	whipping cream (35%)
¼ cup	icing sugar
½ tsp	vanilla
1¼ cups	cream cheese (about one and one-quarter 250 g pkg), softened
¼ cup	graham cracker crumbs
½ cup	fruit preserves (see Tip, below)

How to make it

Halve vanilla bean lengthwise; using tip of sharp knife, scrape seeds into large bowl (save vanilla pod for another use or discard). Add whipping cream, icing sugar and vanilla; beat until soft peaks form. Set aside in refrigerator.

In separate bowl, beat cream cheese until smooth, scraping down side of bowl often; fold in whipped cream, one-third at a time.

Divide half of the cheese mixture among four ½-cup (125 mL) canning jars; top with graham cracker crumbs and half of the fruit preserves. Top with remaining cheese mixture and fruit preserves. Cover and refrigerate until chilled, about 1 hour. (*Make-ahead: Refrigerate for up to 24 hours.*)

MAKES 4 SERVINGS. PER SERVING: about 566 cal, 7 g pro, 42 g total fat (26 g sat. fat), 42 g carb, 1 g fibre, 137 mg chol, 275 mg sodium, 164 mg potassium. % RDI: 9% calcium, 9% iron, 44% vit A, 7% vit C, 8% folate.

Look for home-style fruit preserves to top these mini-cheesecakes. Ones that feature whole berries, pitted cherries or chunks of ripe peach are especially nice with the cream-cheese mixture.

Parfaits are pretty and so easy to make.

Lemon Crunch Parfaits

Creamy lemon curd is the base for these crunchy, sweet treats. If you're a big fan of lemon curd, make a double batch and spread some on toast or scones in the morning.

What you need

¾ cup	whipping cream (35%)
1	can (398 mL) apricot halves in light syrup, drained and quartered

ALMOND CRUNCH:

¼ cup	all-purpose flour
2 tbsp	large-flake rolled oats
1 tbsp	packed brown sugar
2 tbsp	unsalted butter, cubed
2 tbsp	slivered almonds

LEMON CURD:

3	egg yolks
1	egg
⅔ cup	granulated sugar
2 tsp	grated lemon zest
½ cup	lemon juice
Pinch	salt

MAKES 6 SERVINGS. PER SERVING: about 337 cal, 5 g pro, 19 g total fat (10 g sat. fat), 38 g carb, 1 g fibre, 181 mg chol, 29 mg sodium, 165 mg potassium. % RDI: 5% calcium, 7% iron, 26% vit A, 18% vit C, 15% folate.

How to make it

ALMOND CRUNCH: In bowl, stir together flour, oats and brown sugar. Using pastry blender or two knives, cut in butter until crumbly. Stir in almonds. Spread on parchment paper–lined rimmed baking sheet; bake in 350°F (180°C) oven until golden and crisp, about 12 minutes. Let cool.

LEMON CURD: In heatproof bowl, whisk together egg yolks, egg, sugar, lemon zest, lemon juice and salt. Set over saucepan of simmering water; cook, whisking often, until thick enough to coat back of spoon and instant-read thermometer reads 160°F (71°C), 8 to 10 minutes. Strain through fine-mesh sieve into clean bowl; place plastic wrap directly on surface. Refrigerate until cold and set, about 1 hour.

Loosen curd with spoon. Whip cream; fold half into curd. Fold in remaining whipped cream.

Divide apricots among six dessert glasses; divide lemon mixture over top. Sprinkle almond crunch over each.

We've all whipped cream a little too much and ended up with a grainy, curdled mess. If you do, don't throw it out. Stir in a tablespoon or two of unwhipped cream to make it smooth and fluffy again.

Light Berry Fool

A fool is an easy, old-fashioned dessert of whipped cream and fruit. This modern take
is lightened up with yogurt and uses convenient frozen mixed berries.

What you need

1 cup	Balkan-style plain yogurt
¾ cup	whipping cream (35%)
2 tbsp	granulated sugar
Dash	vanilla
1 cup	drained thawed frozen mixed berries
	Fresh mint leaves

How to make it

Line sieve with cheesecloth; set over bowl. Spoon in yogurt; refrigerate until slightly thickened, about 1 hour. Transfer drained yogurt to large bowl; discard liquid.

In separate bowl, whip together cream, sugar and vanilla until soft peaks form; fold into yogurt.

Fold in berries, leaving streaks in yogurt mixture. Spoon into dessert glasses; garnish with mint.

MAKES 4 SERVINGS. PER SERVING: about 246 cal,
3 g pro, 19 g total fat (12 g sat. fat), 16 g carb, 2 g fibre,
68 mg chol, 35 mg sodium, 165 mg potassium. % RDI:
10% calcium, 2% iron, 20% vit A, 18% vit C, 5% folate.

TEST KITCHEN TIP

Folding combines a light mixture with a heavy mixture in such a way that the air cells don't break down and the mixture doesn't deflate or lose volume. This is especially important for a soufflé, sponge cake, angel food cake, génoise or fool. Unlike stirring, folding requires a gentle down-across-up-and-over motion of a spatula to combine the two mixtures without removing the air.

Honey Cream With Vanilla-Roasted Figs

Since honey is the star of this silky cream, use a flavourful variety such as clover, orange blossom or wildflower. Floral honey and grassy thyme are perfect partners.

What you need

2 tbsp	packed brown sugar
1 tbsp	liquid honey
1 tsp	vanilla
½ tsp	chopped fresh thyme
½ tsp	grated lemon zest
Pinch	salt
450 g	fresh figs (such as Black Mission), about 9

HONEY CREAM:

2 cups	whipping cream (35%)
4	egg yolks
⅓ cup	clover or other flavourful liquid honey

How to make it

HONEY CREAM: In heatproof bowl, whisk together 1 cup of the cream, egg yolks and honey. Set bowl over saucepan of simmering water; cook, stirring, until mixture is thick enough to coat back of spoon, about 15 minutes. Strain through fine sieve into large bowl; place plastic wrap directly on surface; let cool. Refrigerate until cold, about 1 hour.

Whip remaining cream; fold into honey mixture. Refrigerate until cold and mixture is thick enough to mound on spoon, 3½ to 4 hours.

Meanwhile, in bowl, stir together brown sugar, honey, vanilla, thyme, lemon zest and salt. Cut figs in half lengthwise and add to bowl; toss to coat. Scrape into 8-inch (2 L) square baking dish; turn figs cut side down. Cover with foil.

Bake in 400°F (200°C) oven until fork-tender, 20 to 25 minutes. Let cool in pan on rack until liquid reabsorbs into figs, about 20 minutes. Serve warm or at room temperature with honey cream.

MAKES 6 SERVINGS. PER SERVING: about 442 cal, 4 g pro, 32 g total fat (19 g sat. fat), 40 g carb, 3 g fibre, 238 mg chol, 37 mg sodium, 280 mg potassium. % RDI: 9% calcium, 6% iron, 31% vit A, 3% vit C, 10% folate.

In a hurry? Serve these roasted figs over vanilla bean ice cream or lightly sweetened full-fat Mediterranean yogurt instead of the honey cream.

Baked Apples With Figs and Almonds

Baked apples are one of those homey desserts no one seems to make anymore.
We're bringing them back—updated with a topping of sweet figs and crunchy almonds.

What you need

4	apples (see Tip, below)
¼ cup	natural almonds (see Tip, page 75)
½ cup	chopped dried Mission figs or pitted prunes
2 tbsp	packed brown sugar
1 tbsp	almond liqueur (such as amaretto) or maple syrup
4 tsp	butter
½ cup	apple juice

How to make it

Using melon baller or spoon, core apples, leaving ¼-inch (5 mm) base. Using fork or tip of sharp knife, pierce skin of each apple four times. Set aside.

On rimmed baking sheet, toast almonds until golden and fragrant, about 10 minutes. Let cool; finely chop.

Stir together almonds, figs, brown sugar and almond liqueur; spoon into apple centres. Top each apple with 1 tsp butter.

Place apples in 8-inch (2 L) square baking dish; pour in apple juice. Bake in 375°F (190°C) oven until tender, about 45 minutes.

MAKES 4 SERVINGS. PER SERVING: about 249 cal, 3 g pro, 9 g total fat (3 g sat. fat), 44 g carb, 6 g fibre, 10 mg chol, 35 mg sodium, 398 mg potassium. % RDI: 6% calcium, 9% iron, 5% vit A, 10% vit C, 3% folate.

TEST KITCHEN TIP

This is another sweet treat that requires cooking or baking apples. Use a variety that will hold up well in the oven, such as Honeycrisp, Royal Gala, Northern Spy, Golden Delicious or Cortland. They're sweet, juicy and sturdy enough to be filled and roasted.

Brown Sugar–Roasted Fall Fruit

Browning the butter lightly before tossing it with the apples and pears
brings a slightly nutty flavour to this beautiful dish. Serve over vanilla ice cream or
frozen yogurt for a rustic, easy finish to a meal.

What you need

3	Royal Gala apples (see Tip, page 144)
3	firm ripe pears (see Tip, below)
1 tbsp	lemon juice
⅔ cup	unsalted butter
¾ cup	packed brown sugar
½ tsp	nutmeg

How to make it

Halve and core apples and pears; cut each half into three wedges. Place in roasting pan; toss with lemon juice.

In small saucepan, melt butter over medium heat until golden and fragrant, 3 to 5 minutes. Add brown sugar, nutmeg and 1 tbsp water; cook, stirring, until sugar is dissolved, about 1 minute. Pour over apple mixture, tossing to coat (mixture will clump).

Roast in 425°F (220°C) oven, turning once halfway through, until fruit is fork-tender and lightly caramelized, about 30 minutes. Serve with pan juices.

MAKES 6 TO 8 SERVINGS. PER EACH OF 8 SERVINGS:
about 277 cal, 1 g pro, 16 g total fat (10 g sat. fat), 37 g carb,
3 g fibre, 41 mg chol, 12 mg sodium, 208 mg potassium. % RDI:
3% calcium, 4% iron, 14% vit A, 7% vit C, 2% folate.

TEST KITCHEN TIP

The best pears for baking are firm and ripe. In The Test Kitchen, we like the flavour and texture of Bartlett and Bosc pears most of all.

Honey-Roasted Pears

You don't need rich sweets all the time. Sometimes you just
want the choicest fruit prepared in the simplest way. These pears celebrate
the fruit's best qualities with a minimum of fuss.

What you need

4	large Bosc pears (about 900 g), see Tip, below
⅓ cup	liquid honey
2 tbsp	butter
2 tbsp	orange juice

FILLING:

½ cup	cream cheese, softened
2 tbsp	liquid honey
1	egg yolk
¼ tsp	grated orange zest

MAKES 4 SERVINGS. PER SERVING: about 393 cal,
4 g pro, 17 g total fat (10 g sat. fat), 61 g carb, 5 g fibre,
98 mg chol, 132 mg sodium. % RDI: 5% calcium, 7% iron,
18% vit A, 17% vit C, 12% folate.

How to make it

FILLING: Beat together cream cheese, honey, egg yolk
and orange zest until smooth. Set aside.

Peel and halve pears, leaving stems intact. Trim thin
slice off each curved side to level. Using melon baller or
teaspoon, remove core and enough of the centre to make
1½-inch (4 cm) wide and ¾-inch (2 cm) deep hollow,
without going through bottom. Place, cut side up,
in well-greased 13- x 9 -inch (3 L) baking dish.

In microwaveable glass measure, heat together ¼ cup of
the honey, butter and orange juice on high until melted,
30 to 45 seconds. Stir; brush all over pears.

Turn pears cut sides down. Bake in 375°F (190°C) oven,
basting every 10 minutes, for 30 minutes. Turn pears and
baste; bake for 10 minutes.

Pour any liquid in centres of pears into baking dish.
Spoon generous 1 tbsp filling into centre of each pear.

In bowl, stir remaining honey with ⅓ cup boiling water.
Stir into liquid in baking dish. Bake, basting once, until
filling is puffed and pears are golden and tender, about
30 minutes. Transfer to platter; spoon sauce over top.

TEST KITCHEN TIP

Bosc pears are ideal for this recipe because they keep their long, elegant
shape and toothsome texture after roasting. Look for ones with golden to
brown skin for the best ripeness.

Roasted Summer Fruit
With Spiced Mascarpone Cream

Mascarpone cheese is rich tasting and has a smooth texture that's ideal
for a creamy mixture like this. Here it's nicely spiced with ginger (and cardamom,
if you like it), which complements the tender caramelized fruit.

What you need

⅓ cup	sliced almonds
2	each apricots and plums, pitted and quartered
2	peaches or nectarines, pitted and quartered
⅓ cup	packed brown sugar
3 tbsp	brandy or apple juice
2 tbsp	butter, melted
1 cup	mascarpone cheese
½ tsp	ground ginger
½ tsp	vanilla
Pinch	ground cardamom (optional)
½ cup	whipping cream (35%)

MAKES 4 SERVINGS. PER SERVING: about 580 cal,
6 g pro, 47 g total fat (27 g sat. fat), 34 g carb, 3 g fibre,
137 mg chol, 76 mg sodium, 378 mg potassium. % RDI:
10% calcium, 7% iron, 38% vit A, 10% vit C, 3% folate.

How to make it

In dry skillet, toast almonds over medium heat, shaking pan often, until light golden, about 5 minutes (see Tip, below). Transfer to plate; let cool.

In small roasting pan or large ovenproof skillet, toss together apricots, plums, peaches, half of the brown sugar, the brandy and butter. Roast in 400°F (200°C) oven, stirring occasionally, until fork-tender, 15 to 20 minutes.

Meanwhile, in bowl, beat together mascarpone cheese, remaining brown sugar, ginger, vanilla, and cardamom (if using) until smooth. Whip cream; fold half into mascarpone mixture. Fold in remaining whipped cream and half of the almonds. *(Make-ahead: Cover and refrigerate fruit and cream separately for up to 4 hours.)*

Mound mascarpone mixture in bowls or dessert dishes. Spoon fruit and pan juices over top; sprinkle with remaining almonds.

Sliced almonds turn golden quickly. Be sure to keep your eye on them and shake the pan often. They can go from perfect to burned in less than a minute. Once they're just right, take them out of the pan immediately to stop the toasting process.

ACKNOWLEDGMENTS

What a sweet project! (Pun intended.) The people involved in creating this book have a passion for simple, homey treats and desserts, so it was such a pleasure rediscovering our favourites and sharing them with you.

Best of all, I got to collaborate with my beloved colleagues in The Canadian Living Test Kitchen: food director **Annabelle Waugh;** senior food specialist **Rheanna Kish;** and food specialists **Irene Fong, Amanda Barnier, Jennifer Bartoli** and **Leah Kuhne.** We reminisced about the greatest crisps and crumbles we've ever tasted, the types of rice pudding our families made, and why Annabelle's recipe for The Best Chocolate Toffee Brownies (page 71) really is the best one you'll ever try. (The secret: toffee bits!) I'd like to thank the women in The Test Kitchen for being consummate professionals and the finest crew anyone could ask to work with.

Next, a huge thank-you to our art director, **Colin Elliott,** who designed this delicious recipe collection. His sharp eye, good taste and keen sense of humour make the process a pleasure—even when deadlines are looming and patience is a virtue in short supply.

Our food looks so good because we work with a pool of very talented photographers, food stylists and prop stylists. They like to celebrate the beauty of our recipes as much as we do. For a full list of the people who created the gorgeous pictures in this volume, turn to page 159.

After the editing and layout of the book are done, two very important people make sure we get all the details right. I'd like to say thanks to our delightful copy editor, **Lisa Fielding,** and our gracious indexer, **Beth Zabloski.** They go through every word, making sure everything is perfect and that the index is helpful and easy to use. I'd also like to thank Sharyn Joliat of Info Access, who creates the nutrient analysis for each of our recipes.

They're a humble bunch, but I'd still like to say *merci beaucoup* to the team at Transcontinental Books: vice-president **Marc Laberge,** publishing director **Mathieu de Lajartre,** sales director **Alain Laberge,** and assistant editors **Céline Comtois** and **Narjisse Ibnattya Andaloussi.** Their hard work makes our jobs easier.

Finally, thanks to *Canadian Living* publisher **Jacqueline Loch,** editorial director **Sandra E. Martin** and tablet publishing manager **Jessica Ross** for their support and dedication to this and many other books.

Tina Anson Mine
Project Editor

Index

Index

CREDITS

Recipes

All recipes developed by The Canadian Living Test Kitchen

Photography

MARK BURSTYN
pages 54 and 95.

JEFF COULSON
back cover (cake and portrait); pages 4,5, 12, 31, 32, 37, 38, 41, 60, 63, 80, 85, 107, 108, 118, 123 and 127.

YVONNE DUIVENVOORDEN
back cover (brownies); pages 6, 7, 9, 16, 22, 44, 64, 73, 76, 92, 102, 137, 139 and 150.

JOE KIM
page 124.

JIM NORTON
back cover (loaf and cobbler); pages 15, 48, 69, 86, 96 and 133.

EDWARD POND
pages 25, 57, 114, 117, 130 and 145.

JODI PUDGE
back cover (parfait); pages 21, 47, 53, 79 and 140.

DAVID SCOTT
page 149.

RYAN SZULC
front cover; pages 28, 70, 91, 101, 111 and 146.

Food Styling

ASHLEY DENTON
front cover; pages 28, 101, 111, 124 and 146.

DAVID GRENIER
pages 41, 63, 80, 91 and 123.

ADELE HAGAN
page 133.

IAN MUGGRIDGE
page 21.

LUCIE RICHARD
back cover (parfait); pages 25, 47, 79, 102, 140, 145 and 149.

CLAIRE STANCER
pages 9, 22 and 64.

CLAIRE STUBBS
back cover (brownies, loaf, cobbler and cake); pages 4, 5, 6, 7, 15, 38, 44, 48, 57, 69, 73, 76, 86, 96, 114, 117, 127, 130, 137, 139 and 150.

MELANIE STUPARYK
pages 12, 85, 107, 108 and 118.

ROSEMARIE SUPERVILLE
pages 16, 54, 92 and 95.

NOAH WITENOFF
pages 31 and 37.

NICOLE YOUNG
pages 32, 53, 60 and 70.

Prop Styling

LAURA BRANSON
front cover; back cover (brownies, loaf and cobbler); pages 15, 21, 28, 48, 73, 76, 86, 96, 101, 108, 111, 124, 133 and 146.

AURELIE BRYCE
pages 41, 63, 80 and 123.

CATHERINE DOHERTY
back cover (parfait and cake); pages 4, 5, 16, 22, 25, 38, 47, 54, 64, 79, 85, 92, 95, 102, 127, 130, 137, 139, 140 and 145.

MADELEINE JOHARI
pages 32, 44, 60, 70, 91 and 118.

SABRINA LINN
pages 12, 31, 37 and 107.

OKSANA SLAVUTYCH
pages 9, 53 and 149.

GENEVIEVE WISEMAN
pages 6, 7, 57, 69, 114, 117 and 150.

ABOUT OUR NUTRITION INFORMATION

To meet nutrient needs each day, moderately active women 25 to 49 need about 1,900 calories, 51 g protein, 261 g carbohydrate, 25 to 35 g fibre and not more than 63 g total fat (21 g saturated fat). Men and teenagers usually need more. Canadian sodium intake of approximately 3,500 mg daily should be reduced, whereas the intake of potassium from food sources should be increased to 4,700 mg per day.

The percentage of recommended daily intake (% RDI) is based on the values used for Canadian food labels for calcium, iron, vitamins A and C, and folate.

Figures are rounded off. They are based on the first ingredient listed when there is a choice and do not include optional ingredients or those with no specified amounts.

ABBREVIATIONS

cal = calories   pro = protein   carb = carbohydrate   sat. fat = saturated fat   chol = cholesterol

Transcontinental Books

Canadian Living

THE CANADIAN LIVING COOKBOOK COLLECTION

Trusted recipes from our Test Kitchen

Find these titles everywhere books are sold or
buy online at **canadianliving.com/books**

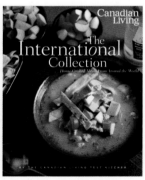